Singapore English

David Deterding

Edinburgh University Press

© David Deterding, 2007

Edinburgh University Press Ltd
22 George Square, Edinburgh

Typeset in 10.5/12 Janson
by Servis Filmsetting Ltd, Manchester, and
printed and bound in Great Britain by
Athenaeum Press, Gateshead

A CIP record for this book is available from the British Library

ISBN 978 0 7486 2544 4 (hardback)
ISBN 978 0 7486 2545 1 (paperback)

'If you are only ever going to read one book about Singapore English, then read this one. The book is logically and clearly presented and a pleasure to read. Readers will obtain a clear description and analysis of the linguistic features of Singapore English, understand the context in which these have developed and be familiar with the controversies surrounding its use.'

Andy Kirkpatrick, Professor and Head of English, Hong Kong Institute of Education

'This remarkably comprehensive volume provides an excellent, informative account of present day Singapore English along with a balanced and insightful discussion of the political and ideological factors involved. As such, it will prove an invaluable resource for all those interested in current developments in World Englishes, teacher and student alike.'

Jennifer Jenkins, Professor of English Language, University of Southampton

Dialects of English

Volumes available in the series
Robert McColl Millar, *Northern and Insular Scots*
978 0 7486 2317 4

David Deterding, *Singapore English*
978 0 7486 2545 1

Forthcoming titles include
Jennifer Hay, Margaret Maclagan and Elizabeth Gordon, *New Zealand English*
978 0 7486 2530 7

Bridget L. Anderson, *Smoky Mountain English*
978 0 7486 3039 4

Sailaja Pingali, *Indian English*
978 0 7486 2595 6

Sandra Clarke, *Newfoundland English*
978 0 7486 2617 5

Contents

1 Introduction

Singapore is a small island in South-East Asia, just off the southern tip of the Malay peninsular, a little over one degree north of the equator. It has a total area of about 650 square kilometres, so it is nearly twice the size of the Isle of Wight in the UK or one fifth the size of Rhode Island in the USA. The population is about 4.3 million, which makes it the second most densely populated country in the world (after Monaco).

Geographically, the main island of Singapore is shaped like a diamond, about 40 kilometres east to west, and 25 kilometres north to south. Most of the island is now built-up, though there is a central reservation area that includes forests and reservoirs in the middle. Singapore's nearest neighbour to the north is Malaysia, to which it is connected by a one-kilometre causeway and also (since 1998) a two-kilometre bridge; its nearest neighbour to the south and west is Indonesia, particularly the small islands of Batam and Bintan to the south and the large island of Sumatra to the west. Historically and culturally, the links with Malaysia have always been strong, and Singapore was briefly a member of the Federation of Malaysia from 1963 to 1965. For a map showing the location of Singapore in relation to its closest neighbours, see Figure 1.1, and for a larger-scale map of Singapore showing the location of some of the places mentioned in this book, see Figure 1.2.

Of the resident population of Singapore in the 2000 census, 77 per cent are ethnically Chinese, 14 per cent are Malay, 8 per cent are Indian, and a little over 1 per cent are classified as 'others' (which includes Eurasians). We should note that the resident population is about 3.5 million, so these figures for the ethnic breakdown exclude about 800,000 temporary residents, including maids, guest workers and expatriate professionals from a wide range of different countries.

Figure 1.1 The location of Singapore in South-East Asia

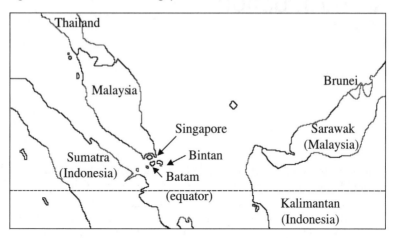

1.1 History

The modern history of Singapore dates from 29 January 1819, when Stamford Raffles landed in the south of the island and established as part of the British Empire a trading post near what is now the Central Business District. Until then, there was just a small population of Malay farmers and fishing folk, but the population soon burgeoned, especially with immigrants from the seaboard Chinese provinces of Fujian and Guangdong, and also some immigrants from India. Although the proportion of Indians has always been small, many of them were teachers, so their influence on the English of Singapore was significant.

Singapore remained a British colony (with a brief but brutal occupation by the Japanese army from 1942 until 1945) until it gained independence in 1963. It then immediately joined the newly-formed Malaysian Federation, but relations between the Singapore administration led by Lee Kuan Yew and the federal government in Kuala Lumpur were somewhat tempestuous, and Singapore left the Federation in 1965. Since then, it has been an independent city-state.

Originally, in 1965, there were widespread concerns about the ability of Singapore to support itself, especially given its almost complete lack of natural resources apart from its people. However, not only has it survived, it has actually thrived over the past four decades, and its per-capita income and standards of living are now among the highest in the world.

Figure 1.2 Map of Singapore, showing some of the places mentioned in the data.

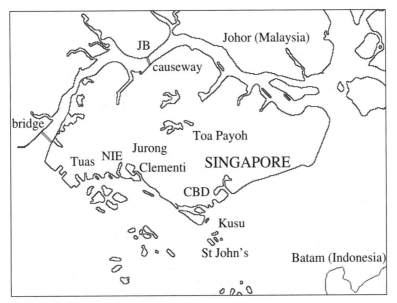

The abbreviations shown on the map are:

NIE: National Institute of Education
CBD: Central Business District
JB: Johor Bahru

1.2 Languages

Traditionally, most of the ethnically Chinese population of Singapore spoke one of the southern varieties of Chinese, particularly Hokkien, Cantonese, Teochew, Hainanese or Hakka. However, in the late 1970s, the government concluded that the use of so many different Chinese dialects was rather divisive, and it was also inefficient for children to speak one language at home and then learn two more – English and Mandarin – at school, so the Speak Mandarin Campaign was launched in 1979 to persuade the Chinese population to use Mandarin instead. This was highly successful, and quite remarkably most Chinese people switched to the use of Mandarin as a home language within a single generation. Nowadays few university undergraduates have an active command of any variety of Chinese other than Mandarin, though many state that they can still understand their traditional dialect moderately well. This has undoubtedly created greater cohesion among the Chinese population and also reduced the learning load of children when they go to school, and furthermore it has enhanced the opportunities for Singaporeans to do business in the People's Republic of China. However, one unfortunate consequence is that many young people can no longer communicate very effectively with their grandparents.

Virtually the entire Malay population speaks Malay, and despite their minority status, the position of the language is not threatened, as a variety of Malay is the national language of both neighbouring countries, Malaysia and Indonesia. Many Malays in Singapore maintain close ties with family in Malaysia and visit them often, and this helps to reinforce the status of Malay in Singapore.

Most of the Indian population originated from South-East India and spoke Tamil, though quite a few also spoke other Indian languages such as Hindi, Gujarati and Mayalayam, and the Sikhs from north India spoke Punjabi. Although Tamil is enshrined as one of the four official languages in Singapore (the others being Mandarin Chinese, Malay and English), its status as a minority language and the lack of support from neighbouring countries means that many young Singaporeans of Indian descent no longer have an active command of their ethnic language.

Virtually everyone in Singapore speaks some English, and it can perhaps claim to be the only country in Asia where this is true. In fact, one can pretty much guarantee to be able to communicate quite easily and effectively in English even when talking to a taxi driver or buying things in a local shop. Since 1987, the primary medium of all education has been English, and about 30 per cent of the population now predominantly speak English at home, with this proportion gradually increasing every year: Ministry of Education figures claim that 50 per cent of school-age children now speak English as their main home language. Of course, the variety of English spoken in Singapore is not the same as that found in other countries such as Britain, the USA or Australia, and a detailed description of the unique flavour of Singapore English is the topic of this book.

The government actively promotes a bilingual policy, so all school children are supposed to become proficient in English and one other language, generally Mandarin Chinese, Malay or Tamil. There are now provisions for some children to select a less challenging syllabus for their second language (officially termed their 'mother tongue'), so that, for example, there is now a less demanding Chinese syllabus for those students who struggle to attain a first-language mastery in Mandarin, but a good command of English is regarded as essential for everyone.

Even if not everyone achieves complete mastery in both their languages, nearly all children do achieve basic competency and reasonable fluency in two languages. What is remarkable is that all four official languages – English, Mandarin Chinese, Malay and Tamil – belong to entirely different language families: English is Indo-European, Chinese is Sino-Tibetan, Malay is Austronesian, and Tamil is Dravidian. This situation, where nearly everyone grows up speaking two of four official languages none of which is even remotely related to any other of the four, must be unique in the world. Linguistically, Singapore is evidently very special.

1.3 Varieties of Singapore English

Singapore is too small for any real regional variation in English to have emerged, especially as the government insists that all housing estates must be racially mixed, to prevent ethnic ghettos becoming established. However, there is substantial variation in the language, both along ethnic and educational lines.

Most Singaporeans can immediately guess the ethnic background of a Singaporean speaker, and Deterding and Poedjosoedarmo (2000) show that listeners can achieve a 90 per cent accuracy rate in deciding whether an undergraduate speaker is Malay or Chinese on the basis of just ten seconds of conversational English. However, while it is certainly true that the spoken English of Chinese Singaporeans is distinct from that of Malay or Indian Singaporeans, at the same time many features of the language are shared by the different ethnic groups. For example: for pronunciation, Deterding (2005b) shows that *egg* rhymes with *vague* but not with *peg* for nearly everyone, regardless of their ethnic background; for syntax, both Chinese and Malay Singaporeans frequently use *will* to refer to a regular event and *would* to express tentativeness, as we will see in Chapter 3; and for the lexicon, all races use borrowed words such as *kiasu* ('afraid to lose out', from Hokkien) and *makan* ('eat', from Malay). So it appears that a distinct brand of Singapore English is emerging, common to all the ethnic groups living in the country and quite unlike the varieties of English found in most other parts of the world, though it is true that many of its features are shared with the English spoken in Malaysia. It seems likely that the main difference between the English of the various ethnic groups in Singapore lies in the intonation (Lim 2000), though the precise details of the intonation of the different groups have yet to be established.

The greatest variation in English is undoubtedly between educated Singapore English and colloquial Singapore English (popularly known as 'Singlish'). There is some debate about whether these varieties exist along a continuum (Pakir 1991) or whether a diglossic situation exists between them, involving a clear switch between the two styles of speech according to the situation in which the interaction takes place (Gupta 1992a). What is certainly true is that many young people can easily switch between the two varieties depending on who they are talking to, where they are, and what they are talking about. However, it is still uncertain if the two varieties really are clearly separate, as in a classic diglossic situation like Tamil or Arabic, where a distinct version of the language is adopted in formal circumstances such as public speeches, religious services, and the classroom. The issue of separate varieties of Singapore English and how they are described will be discussed in more depth in Chapter 5.

1.4 Variation in the data

The substantial variation in the English found in Singapore constitutes a problem when we are attempting to describe the language. In effect, whenever we present illustrative examples, comprehensive details should be given about the speakers, including their age, ethnic background and level of education, as well as the circumstances surrounding the speech, such as the venue, who the listeners were and what the topic was. All of those factors have a substantial influence on the style of speech that is adopted.

In this book, the problems of variation are dealt with by basing the analysis mostly on the speech of one ethnically Chinese female university undergraduate recorded on a single occasion while she was being interviewed by her close friend. While this approach obviously fails to capture the range of Singapore English, it does allow us to describe a coherent variety of the language in some detail. Furthermore, it enables us to conduct a substantial investigation into the occurrence of certain features, including the influences from the phonological environment on particular aspects of pronunciation and also the frequency of occurrence of certain words and grammatical structures, without being concerned about variation in style or speaking environment.

One danger with this approach is that the speaker might have idiosyncratic patterns that are not in fact common among the general population. However, for the most part we are not attempting to discover new patterns of speech but instead we are presenting illustrative materials for features that are already widely known, so it is unlikely that we will be misled by the unusual patterns of this speaker. We must acknowledge, though, that the speaker almost certainly does use some words and exhibit some features of pronunciation more frequently than other speakers, and also that the patterns of occurrence for some grammatical structures which are described here might not be shared by other Singaporeans.

It is, of course, unfortunate that almost no data is presented on the speech of Malays or Indians, or of people with less advanced levels of education, and furthermore that we do not include material from casual conversations in truly informal settings. However, the data here do serve rather well to illustrate most of the features of Singapore English that have been described in the literature, especially for pronunciation, and in fact in Chapter 2, on phonetics and phonology, only data from this single speaker will be presented. In Chapters 3 and 4, where examples are lacking for certain features of syntax and lexis, some other materials will be included, from the National Institute of Education Corpus of Spoken Singapore English (NIECSSE) and also from recent blogs written by Singaporeans. Here, we will first describe the data from the main speaker, who we will refer to as Hui Min (not her real name), and then we will discuss the NIECSSE data and also the use of blogs.

1.5 Data from Hui Min

The main subject is a thirty-four-year-old ethnically Chinese, female, Singaporean undergraduate. At the time of the recording, she was in her Honours year at the National Institute of Education (NIE) in Singapore, where English was one of her teaching subjects as well as her chosen speciality. She reported that English is now her best language, though until the age of seven she spoke mainly Teochew and Mandarin to her parents, grandparents, sisters and brother, and she still sometimes talks to her family and friends in Mandarin.

The original purpose of the recording was to collect data for an investigation into extra final consonants. For an Honours Year research project, Lim Siew Hwee, a student in the English Language and Literature Academic Group at NIE, became interested in the occurrence of these extra consonants, particularly a [t] that sometimes appears on the end of words such as *in*, *house* and *yes*, and she noticed that three of the subjects from the NIECSSE data (F9, F10 and F13) exhibited this phenomenon quite often when they were being interviewed by their academic tutor. So she arranged for these three subjects to be interviewed by their close friends, to see if the extra consonants would similarly occur in a more casual situation than the relatively formal interviews that constitute the NIECSSE recordings. The findings of this research are presented in detail in Lim (2003) and summarised in Lim and Deterding (2005), and the data for all three subjects is available in the Lim Siew Hwee Corpus of Informal Singapore Speech (Deterding and Lim 2005). Hui Min is one of those three subjects, and she was selected for the current study because her speech is the clearest and the most extensive of the three. She is numbered F13 in the NIECSSE data and iF13 in the Lim Siew Hwee corpus (with the 'i' indicating that it is her informal data). All extracts of the informal data presented here are tagged as iF13, though she will be referred to as Hui Min in the text of the book.

The recording was made directly onto a computer in the Phonetics Laboratory at NIE, with a high-quality Shure SM48 dynamic microphone placed a few centimetres from the mouth of the subject. This ensures that her voice is always loud and clear, though the occasional questions from the interviewer are much fainter. Inevitably, the setting in the Phonetics Laboratory and the somewhat intrusive nature of the microphone to some extent prevent the conversation becoming truly informal. It is one of the unfortunate aspects of data collection that, in order to ensure a high-quality recording and thereby allow detailed phonetic analysis, it is necessary to use a good microphone placed close to the speaker, and this inevitably interferes with the naturalness of the speech. This is sometimes called the observer's paradox: one can never observe something in detail without actually changing it. Many large-scale corpora, such as the ICE corpus (Nelson et al. 2002), include truly informal data recorded in a home setting or in restaurants and pubs using a fairly unobtrusive microphone, but much of the speech is exceptionally noisy and not suited for detailed phonetic research. And when Carter and McCarthy (2006) wanted to provide audio samples of genuine conversational data from the CANCODE Corpus to illustrate real language usage for their Cambridge Grammar of English, they had actors re-record the data, as the original recordings were too noisy.

Here the data of Hui Min is presented in its original form. Although it must be admitted that the speech is not entirely natural or completely informal, it does represent a remarkable resource for the description of Singapore English. The speaker is exceptionally clear and highly articulate, but at the same time her speech is distinctly Singaporean. As an extensive sample of educated Singapore English speech, it provides an extraordinarily valuable source of data.

The data for Hui Min consists of twelve separate parts, each lasting five minutes, so the total duration of the recording is exactly one hour. Each part is in a separate .WAV file, labelled 'iF13' followed by 'a', 'b', 'c', and so on, and the full orthographic transcripts of these twelve files are included in Chapter 7. In the illustrative data included in the main chapters of this book, all extracts from her speech are tagged with the file number followed by its location in seconds from the start of the file. It is hoped that readers will be able to listen to the data in the dedicated website (http://www.lel.ed.ac.uk/dialects/) as they read the text, and they may furthermore choose to listen to all of the data from Hui Min, to gain a genuine sense of what educated Singapore English sounds like.

1.6 Data from NIECSSE

The one-hour recording of Hui Min is sufficient to provide a comprehensive analysis of the phonology of the educated Singapore English of an ethnically Chinese speaker. However, it is not quite enough to offer examples of all syntactic and lexical phenomena that have often been described in the literature. Therefore, in Chapters 3 and 4, supplementary data will be used from the National Institute of Education Corpus of Spoken Singapore English (NIECSSE). This consists of forty-six interviews lasting five minutes each of educated young Singaporeans – thirty-one female and fifteen male – by a British university lecturer (the author of this book). Nearly all of the Singaporeans were trainee teachers at NIE at the time of the recording, and most were about to start a course on Experimental Phonetics for which the interviewer was the lecturer and tutor. All the interviews began with the question 'What did you do in your last vacation?', and then the conversation progressed to other topics, such as previous holidays and plans for the future. The recordings were all made in the Phonetics Laboratory at NIE, and the recording conditions were the same as for Hui Min. Most of the speakers are Chinese, though four females are Malay (F4, F6, F7 and F16), one is Sikh/Chinese (F8), one is Eurasian (F19) and one male is Indian (M15). Full details of the NIECSSE recordings can be found in Deterding and Low (2005).

All the subjects are well educated and have an excellent ability in English. Most were training to be teachers and English was one of their chosen specialisations during their studies at NIE. When NIECSSE extracts are presented in this book, it can be assumed that the speaker is Chinese unless it is explicitly stated otherwise. Their speech can be described as educated Singapore English and is similar in style to that of Hui Min, though it is rather more formal because the interviewer for the NIECSSE data is an expatriate member of the academic staff at NIE and not a close friend of the speakers.

All the recordings from both Hui Min and NIECSSE are interviews, and this means that some styles of speech do not occur. For example, there are very few questions asked by the subjects, and there are no instances of pleading, cajoling, cursing, chastising or teasing. As a result, it will not be possible to provide a comprehensive description of some aspects of Singapore English, and, for example, we do not find a full range of the discourse particles such as *lah* that have sometimes been observed. (This will be discussed further in Chapter 4.) However, these two sources of data do provide an excellent resource to illustrate most of the features of spoken Singapore English described in this book.

1.7 Data from blogs

According to *The Straits Times* (7 July 2006), there are currently 22,000 bloggers in Singapore, so their output can provide an incredibly rich source of up-to-date data on current language usage. All blogs referred to in this book were accessed using the Technorati search engine.

Of course, blogs are often far more informal than the educated Singapore English used by Hui Min and the NIECSSE speakers, but they do serve to complement those sources of data, especially in areas such as syntax and lexical usage where the one-hour interview of Hui Min and the four hours of NIECCSE data do not provide examples of all the issues we want to discuss. Attempts have been made only to use blogs written mostly in standard English, so those with excessive use of SMS-style abbreviations or innovative spelling and grammar have been avoided.

A number of issues remain with using blogs, including who wrote them and how we should reference them. To ensure that they really are written by Singaporeans, we can either look at the biographical information (when that is provided) or check the content, and it is usually thereby quite easy to determine the source, though of course one can never be certain that all bloggers are telling the truth. Each blog that is quoted in this book is referred to by the writer (wherever possible) and the date of the posting, and the full web addresses are provided at the end of the Bibliography in Chapter 6.

When Gupta (2006) investigated current Singlish usage on the web partly based on blogs, she used the keyword *kiasu*, which is a word borrowed from Hokkien meaning 'fear of losing out' and is often used to describe Singaporean behaviour such as overeating at a buffet to ensure one gets one's full money's worth (Brown 1999: 123). However, use of *kiasu* as a keyword threw up some data from Malaysia as well as Singapore. Here, the blogs were searched using *Singapore* as a keyword. Inevitably, this results in some entries from visitors to Singapore and others written by bloggers from elsewhere commenting on things in Singapore, but it is not difficult to discount these. Here, we are just looking for data to illustrate certain features, and it is mostly quite straightforward to find such examples and to confirm that they were indeed written by Singaporeans, even though full biographical details of the writers, including age, education and ethnic background, are generally not available.

In accessing blogs in this book, we are not attempting to obtain a fully representative sample of language usage. The latter is a more daunting task, though one hopes that one day, perhaps sometime in the near future, instant lexical analyses including detailed tabulated concordances can be achieved from web-based corpora of data such as blogs. When this becomes possible, we will be able to obtain truly up-to-date snapshots of how English is being used, though no doubt web-based analyses will give rise to many outraged howls of protest about the corruption and degeneration of the language. The issue of whether standards of English in Singapore really are falling is discussed further in Chapter 5.

1.8 Outline of the book

We will start with a consideration of pronunciation in Chapter 2, basing the analysis entirely on the data of Hui Min. Chapter 3 then looks at morphology and syntax, while Chapter 4 considers discourse and lexis. In both these chapters, data from Hui Min will be used wherever possible, but examples from NIECSSE and blogs will also be used where necessary. Chapter 5 discusses the history of English in Singapore and also the current situation. Finally, there is an annotated bibliography of works on Singapore English in Chapter 6 and the full transcript of the data for Hui Min is presented in Chapter 7.

2 Phonetics and Phonology

In this chapter, first the consonants and then the vowels of Singapore English will be discussed before we consider suprasegmental features such as rhythm, intonation and stress placement. We will also attempt to compare the sounds of Singapore English with the English found in other countries in the region.

It is important to describe the phonology of each variety of a language on its own terms, without reference to external norms and preconceived notions of how certain words 'should' be pronounced. To this end, we will discuss the vowels of Singapore English by means of the lexical keywords suggested by Wells (1982) and listed in Table 2.1.

Following Wee (2004a), an extra keyword POOR is adopted, as in Singapore the vowel in *poor, sure* and *tour* is different from that in *cure* and *pure*. We will consider issues such as this, as well as mergers like that between FLEECE and KIT and also the quality of the vowel in FACE and GOAT, later in this chapter.

It is important to establish that, in this chapter and elsewhere, we are often talking about tendencies, not absolutes. Many of the features that are discussed are ones that sometimes occur, but there is no suggestion that they are always found, even with data from one speaker recorded on a single occasion. For example, if we say that final pronouns tend to be stressed, we do not claim that they are always stressed, just that they are stressed more often than might be expected in many other varieties of English.

The indeterminate occurrence of some of the features may partly arise because of the emergent status of Singapore English: it is still developing into a mature variety with its own standards which have yet to become fully established, and this may result in an extra element of instability. However, we should also acknowledge that language variation is in fact endemic in all societies, as was demonstrated long ago by Labov (1966). Inherent variation in the pronunciation of words will be

Table 2.1 Lexical keywords and their pronunciation in Singapore English.

FLEECE	i	NURSE	ə	GOAT	o	GOOSE	u
KIT	i	lettER	ə	THOUGHT	ɔ	FOOT	u
happY	i	commA	ə	FORCE	ɔ	PRICE	ai
FACE	e	START	ʌ	NORTH	ɔ	MOUTH	au
DRESS	ɛ	PALM	ʌ	LOT	ɔ	CHOICE	ɔi
TRAP	ɛ	BATH	ʌ	CLOTH	ɔ	NEAR	iə
SQUARE	ɛ	STRUT	ʌ	CURE	ɔ	POOR	uə

illustrated in the first feature that we discuss: the sporadic occurrence of dental fricatives.

2.1 Dental fricatives

Perhaps the most salient segmental feature of Singapore pronunciation, the one that Singaporeans themselves are most likely to be aware of, is the tendency for [t] sometimes to be used instead of [θ], and [d] sometimes to be used in place of [ð] in words which start with 'th', with the result that *tree* and *three* are often homophones, and so are *den* and *then*. Although some speakers never use dental fricatives, Moorthy and Deterding (2000) have shown that, for educated speakers such as most university undergraduates, the occurrence of [θ] or [t] in words such as *three* and *thing* is variable, and also that sometimes a sound intermediate between [θ] and [t] may be used. In addition, they report that in many cases, even trained phoneticians cannot agree on what sound has occurred, and furthermore that acoustic analysis is not much help, as there are a whole range of acoustic cues which combine to influence the perception of the sound.

As expected, Hui Min exhibits variable use of [θ] and [t] in content words that begin with 'th'. Extract 1 illustrates the use of [t] at the start of *things*, and extract 2 reveals her using [θ] in *three* just a few seconds later.

(1) I did quite a few things [tiŋs] during the weekends   {iF13-a:06}

(2) for the past three [θri] weeks   {iF13-a:11}

Similarly, in extract 3 *think* has [t] at the start, but later in the same utterance *three* has [θ]. The fact that [θ] occurs in the tokens of *three* in both extracts 2 and 3 raises the question whether the incidence of [θ] or [t] may be partly lexical, depending on which words are being spoken. This issue will be investigated below.

(3) but I don't think [tiŋ] I . . . I I . . . am able to give them that much in
    three [θri] weeks ah   {iF13-a:201}

For function words beginning with 'th' such as *then* and *that*, [d] is often
used, for example in *then* in extract 4, though [ð] also sometimes occurs,
such as with *that's* in extract 5.

(4) then [dɛn] later on in the evening   {iF13-a:30}

(5) I guess that's [ðɛts] cheap enough   {iF13-a:48}

There is similar variability in the occurrence of the dental fricatives
in the middle of words. In extract 6 [d] occurs in *mother*, but in extract 7
[ð] occurs.

(6) my mother [mʌdə] to look after my nephews   {iF13-k:224}

(7) I tried learning from my mother [mʌðə]   {iF13-l:188}

In syllable-final position, [f] is used instead of [θ], as illustrated in
extracts 8 and 9, though this is also variable, as seen in the occurrence of
[θ] in extract 10.

(8) my sister just gave birth [bəf] to a baby   {iF13-k:119}

(9) Perth [pəf] is a very um quiet place I guess   {iF13-d:83}

(10) I've been to Sydney . . . and Perth [pəθ]   {iF13-d:06}

Interestingly, even though Singaporeans themselves often use [f]
instead of [θ] in final position, if [f] occurs in place of [θ] in initial
position, as is common with speakers from London and also nowadays
with many young speakers from elsewhere in Britain, this can cause
severe problems for comprehension in Singapore. For example, when
Singaporeans attempted to write down what was said in a recording of a
speaker of what is sometimes called 'Estuary English' (the style of
speech which is influenced by the London accent and is now popular in
the south of England), they transcribed *three* that was pronounced with
an initial [f] as 'free', even when this made absolutely no sense in context
(Deterding 2005a).
    One exception to the rule that [f] may occur instead of [θ] at the end
of words is *maths*, which is [mɛts], as in extract 11. It is possible that this
arises because *maths* is related to *mathematics*, and if this word has four
syllables (as in the first pronunciation listed in Wells 2000), then the 'th'

is at the start of the second syllable. An alternative explanation is that [t] rather than [f] occurs in *maths* to avoid the sequence of two fricatives [fs] together.

(11) that's why I chose English and not maths [mɛts]   {iF13-g:96}

2.2 Incidence of [t] or [f] for [θ]

In considering the frequency of occurrence of dental fricatives, we will focus on potential instances of [θ], as [ð] mostly occurs at the start of function words which tend not to be stressed, making it hard to determine what sound occurs.

In the one hour of data for Hui Min, there are 106 tokens of words where 'th' might potentially be pronounced as [θ], and the occurrence of [θ], [t] and [f] in these words is summarised in Table 2.2. Just under half of the tokens with potential [θ] at the start of the word have [t], while nine out of eleven of the tokens with potential [θ] in the middle of a word have [t]. For final [θ], half the tokens have [f], and every single instance of *maths* has [t] (or glottal stop – no attempt was made to differentiate between [t] and [ʔ] in *maths*).

If we consider just the first two rows, we find that out of the eighty-two tokens of initial and medial potential [θ], forty-three tokens (52 per cent) have [t]. This is rather similar to the figure of 49 per cent reported by Moorthy and Deterding (2000) for the informal speech of five university undergraduates (though that study also allowed another category of 'other' for indeterminate tokens).

Let us now consider whether the incidence of [t] or [θ] depends on the identity of the lexical item. Table 2.3 shows the words with potential [θ] in initial and medial position, ordered in terms of their frequency of occurrence in the data for Hui Min.

Table 2.3 suggests that the more common a word is, the more likely it is to have [θ], so the majority of the two most common items, *think(ing)* and *three* have [θ] while most of the other words are more likely to have [t]. However, these results may be distorted by the 17 tokens of *I think*,

Table 2.2 Pronunciation of words with potential [θ].

Position	Examples	[θ]	[t]	[f]	Total
initial	*thing, three*	37	34		71
medial	*something, enthusiasm*	2	9		11
final	*birth, both*	5		5	10
(maths)	*maths*		14		14

Table 2.3 Pronunciation of initial and medial potential [θ] for different words.

Examples	[θ]	[t]	Total
think, thinking	19	9	28
three	11	7	18
thing, things	6	11	17
thirty	0	5	5
something	1	4	5
nothing	0	3	3
enthusiasm, enthusiastic	0	2	2
thought	1	1	2
thirteen	0	1	1
anything	1	0	1
Total	39	43	82

Table 2.4 Pronunciation of potential word-initial [θ] according to the previous sound.

Previous sound	[θ]	[t]	Total
vowel	8	12	20
consonant	15	14	29
pause	0	5	5
I think	14	3	17
Total	37	34	71

all but three of which have [θ], as it is possible that this phrase acts as a unit and behaves differently from other words. Table 2.4 shows the sound that occurs in words with potential initial [θ] according to the previous sound, with *I think* shown separately. These figures suggest that [t] generally occurs after a pause but otherwise that, apart from the common use of [θ] in *I think*, there is no clear influence from the preceding sound.

Here we have considered the position of a potential [θ] in the word, what word it is, and what precedes it. Of course, there are many other possible influences, such as whether the word is repeated or is the first instance, whether it occurs towards the start or end of an utterance, the degree of stress on it, and speaking rate. Investigation of all these potential factors is not feasible here, but what does seem to be clear is that the occurrence of [θ] is variable, and one of the few constants is that *maths* always has a [t] (or glottal stop). We will now compare the situation in Singapore with that in other countries in the region.

2.3 Dental fricatives in South-East Asia

Dental fricatives are, of course, avoided by many speakers of English. This occurs even in traditional English-speaking countries, so Londoners as well as some young people from elsewhere in Britain often use [f] and [v] in place of [θ] and [ð], and many speakers in Ireland and also New York use [t] and [d] (or sometimes dental plosives) (Wells 1982: 328, 429, 515).

In South-East and East Asia, patterns vary. Just like for Singapore, in Malaysia [t] and [d] are found in place of [θ] and [ð] (Baskaran 2004a), and the same is found in Brunei (Mossop 1996), the Philippines (Tayao 2004), and indeed in most of the countries in South-East Asia (Deterding and Kirkpatrick 2006). But in Hong Kong, [f] and [v] tend to be used (Hung 2000), and in Mainland China, [s] tends to be used in place of [θ] while either [d] or [z] may occur instead of [ð], depending on where the speaker comes from (Deterding 2006a).

It is interesting to note that although the populations of Singapore, Hong Kong and Mainland China are all predominantly ethnically Chinese, the pattern of replacement for dental fricatives varies in these three places. In contrast, although the people in the other South-East Asian countries speak a wide range of languages, [t] and [d] are generally found in place of [θ] and [ð]. Contrastive analysis is a technique sometimes used by linguists to compare the sounds that occur in two languages and thereby predict which sounds will be problematic for speakers of one language learning the other, and we might note that although this technique can correctly predict that dental fricatives will be avoided by many learners of English and also maybe by speakers of new varieties of English, it cannot tell what sounds will be adopted as the replacements.

2.4 Final consonant cluster simplification

In Singapore, sequences of more than one consonant, or 'consonant clusters', tend to be simplified when they occur at the end of a word, usually by omitting the final consonant. In fact, the omission of [t] or [d] from the end of a syllable-final consonant cluster happens in most varieties of English, including RP British English broadcast by the BBC (Deterding 2006b), but in her analysis of Singapore data from the NIECSSE corpus, Gut (2005) reports that the incidence of final consonant cluster simplification is rather higher than that found in RP.

In recordings from the BBC, the deletion of plosives [t] and [d] from final consonant clusters is most common when the next word begins with a consonant, especially a plosive such as [p] or [k] or the nasals [m] and [n]. However, in Singapore English, deletion of a final plosive can occur quite often before a word beginning with a vowel, such as the [t] from *first* in extract 12.

(12) during my free time, first [fəs] of all I want to have enough rest [rɛst] ... yah like ... {iF13-b:04}

One reason for this is the relative lack of linking between words, as the final [t] in *first* might be used to link to the next word in many other varieties of English. The lack of linking between words is one factor that contributes to the perception of Singapore English rhythm as being syllable-based, as we will see below.

In extract 12, we can further note that there is variability even within a single utterance, as the final [t] in *rest* is not deleted. A similar example is extract 13, where the [d] in *world* is deleted but the [t] in *environment* is retained.

(13) world [wəl] environment [envaɪrəmənt] ... yah {iF13-b:171}

Other consonants in addition to the alveolar plosives [t] and [d] can be deleted. The final [k] is omitted from *ask* in extract 14 and *think* in 15, even though in both cases the next word begins with a vowel.

(14) students can just ask [ʌs] any questions about ... anything {iF13-h:233}

(15) so after that I think [θiŋ] I have a phobia {iF13-i:181}

2.5 Extra final [t]

In the description of Singapore English, most analyses discuss omitted consonants, but less attention is usually given to added consonants, even though this phenomenon is actually quite common. In fact, as was discussed in Chapter 1, the original purpose of recording the one-hour interview with Hui Min was to investigate this phenomenon.

Extract 16 illustrates instances of extra [t]s, both after *jump* and after *in*. The first of these can be analysed as an -*ed* suffix, so the word might be represented as *jumped*. Even though it occurs after *to* and so one might expect the base form of the verb without a past-tense suffix, there is a pause between *to* and the verb. Maybe the speaker changed her mind about what she wanted to say, so she ignored the *has to* and then used a past tense for *jumped*. However, the extra [t] after *in* is harder to explain.

(16) I couldn't get my feet on the . . . on the ground so in the end the the
      instructor has to . . . jump(ed) [dʒʌmpt] in [int] and then erm . . . pick
      me up mmm   {iF13-i:171}

This extra [t] occurs surprisingly often not just in Singapore English
but in Hong Kong as well (Setter and Deterding 2003). The reasons
behind it are not entirely clear, but Lim and Deterding (2005) suggest it
is a spurious -*ed* suffix that occurs even in unexpected words like *in*. An
alternative articulatory explanation is also possible, as this extra [t]
seems to occur most commonly after [n], so it might be related somehow
to the release of this nasal stop. However, the earlier studies showed that
[t] sometimes occurs after [s] and also occasionally after other consonants such as [m] as well as vowels, so a spurious suffix seems the most
likely explanation.

2.6 Final glottal stop

A glottal stop, the silent catch in the throat that occurs in the middle of
utterances such as *uh-uh*, tends to be used in Singapore English in place
of final plosives when they are not part of a cluster, especially [t] and [k].
In extract 17, a glottal stop is found at the end of both *put* and *heart*, even
though the next word in each case begins with a vowel, and also in *not*
which occurs before a pause; in extract 18, there is a glottal stop at the
end of both *quite* and *lot*; and in extract 19, a glottal stop is found in place
of the final [k] in *back*.

(17) to . . . put [puʔ] all my heart [hʌʔ] in there or . . . or or . . . or not [nɔʔ]
      . . . and then   {iF13-a:154}

(18) which require . . . quite [kwaɪʔ] a lot of [lɔʔɔ] attention
                                                             {iF13-a:194}

(19) likelihood I would not [nɔʔ] request back [bɛʔ] again   {iF13-g:226}

A glottal stop is also increasingly common in many varieties of British
English, including London, East Anglia and Scotland (Wells 1982: 323,
341, 409). In fact, many speakers in Britain also use a glottal stop in
the middle of words like *water* and *butter*, but this occurrence between
two vowels in the middle of a word never occurs in Singapore, and
Singaporeans have considerable difficulty understanding a word like *city*
if a glottal stop is used in place of the [t] (Deterding 2005a). It is interesting to note that the phrase *a lot of* with a glottal stop in the middle is
common in Singapore, as illustrated by extract 18 above, but a glottal

stop never occurs between two vowels in the middle of a word. The problems for comprehension caused by use of a medial glottal stop are rather similar to the substitution of [f] for [θ] discussed above: even though this replacement is also found in Singapore English at the end of words (such as *Perth* and *birth*), its occurrence can interfere with intelligibility if it happens in an unexpected environment (such as at the start of a word like *three*).

2.7 Aspiration

There is sometimes minimal aspiration on an initial voiceless plosive, with the result that [t] sometimes sounds a bit like a [d] in British or American English, and similarly [p] may sound like [b], as in extract 20.

(20) reading the newspaper [njusbebə] more   {iF13-b:59}

Deterding and Poedjoseodarmo (1998: 157) have suggested that this may be an influence from Malay, and in fact it may occur rather more commonly with Malay speakers than someone who is ethnically Chinese like Hui Min.

2.8 Vocalised [l]

There is a tendency in Singapore for dark [l], the sound that occurs in most varieties of English at the end of words such as *school* and before a consonant in words such as *cold*, to be produced as a vowel, or 'vocalised'. When a dark [l] is vocalised in this way, there is actually no contact between the tongue and the roof of the mouth as would usually be expected for a lateral consonant. For Singapore English, Tan (2005) shows that about 65 per cent of tokens of dark [l] in data from the NIECSSE corpus are vocalised, though some speakers use a vocalised [l] more than others.

In extract 21, there is no change in quality at the end of *school* to suggest any kind of residual consonantal gesture for a final [l], and similarly for both *school* and *small* in extract 22, even though *small* is stressed and lengthened. In fact, we might conclude that the dark [l] in these two instances is not just vocalised but actually deleted.

(21) the school [sku] that I'm posted to   {iF13-a:255}

(22) but I guess what I don't like about the school [sku] is the canteen, it's too small [smɔː]   {iF13-f:98}

As a result of deletion of a dark [l] after back vowels, pairs of words such as *wolf~woof* and *tool~two* can end up as homophones in Singapore. Dark [l] may also be deleted after a schwa as in *functional* in extract 23 (where a syllabic [l] does not occur in Singapore English), and as a result *little~litter* may be homophones.

(23) functional [fʌŋʃənə] grammar   {iF13-a:96}

However, after front vowels the vocalised [l] is pronounced as a back vowel rather than deleted, so *wheel* in extract 24 does not sound the same as *wee*.

(24) initially want to take the ferris wheel [wiu]   {iF13-a:73}

Vocalisation of dark [l] (though not generally its deletion) is also extremely common in many varieties of British English, particularly Estuary English (Cruttenden 2001: 88), and Wells (1982: 259) suggests that it may one day become standard. Furthermore, in all varieties of English the historical [l] that once occurred in *folk, calm, should* and *walk* is no longer pronounced, so maybe by deleting the dark [l] after back vowels, Singapore is at the forefront of an on-going historical process.

2.9 Non-prevocalic [r]

In many varieties of English, including RP British English, and the Englishes of Australia, New Zealand and South Africa, an [r] can only occur before a vowel (it must be prevocalic), and this is the usual pattern in Singapore. In contrast, in most varieties of American and Scottish English, an [r] is pronounced wherever it occurs in the spelling, including at the end of a word (as in *car*) or before another consonant (as in *park*). This use of non-prevocalic [r] seems to be becoming increasingly common among Singaporeans, perhaps as an influence from Hollywood and also the American music industry (Poedjosoedarmo 2000b), and it seems to be regarded as 'cool' by many young people in Singapore. Hui Min does not generally use non-prevocalic [r], but just occasionally it does appear, as in extracts 25 and 26.

(25) worked there for [fɔr] . . . six and a half years   {iF13-e:144}

(26) for making erm VCR [visiʌr]   {iF13-e:66}

2.10 Labiodental [r]

A labiodental [r], represented by the phonetic symbol [ʋ], is the [w]-like sound that is sometimes regarded as a speech defect but is actually found among an increasingly widespread range of people in Britain (Foulkes and Docherty 2000). It is not usually reported to occur in Singapore, but Kwek (2005) has shown that, in fact, it does occur, and furthermore that Singaporeans are subconsciously affected by its occurrence, judging speakers who use it to be 'weak' even though they cannot explain why they make that judgement.

Labiodental [r] occasionally occurs in the speech of Hui Min, especially between two vowels such as with *very* in extract 27.

(27) it's definitely very [veʋi] challenging   {iF13-e:243}

2.11 Vowel length

The most widely described feature of the vowel system of Singapore English is the absence of a length distinction between pairs of vowels, so that *beat~bit* tend to sound the same, and so do *pool~pull*, *sports~spots* and *cart~cut*. This is the system of vowels we assumed in Table 2.1 at the start of this chapter, where FLEECE and KIT were both shown with the same vowel [i], GOOSE and FOOT both have [u], THOUGHT, FORCE, NORTH, LOT and CLOTH all have [ɔ], and START, PALM, BATH and STRUT all have [ʌ]. We will now examine the extent to which these mergers are found in the data of Hui Min.

In extract 28, there are four tokens from the FLEECE lexical set, and there is some variation among them, as the vowel in *mean* and the first syllable of *easy* is closer than that in *seen* and *seems* (so the latter two are shown with the more central vowel [ɪ]). Furthermore, in extract 29, *seen* has the same quality as in extract 28, and in extract 30, the first syllable of *scenic* also has [ɪ].

(28) I mean [min] I've seen [sɪn] people rollerblading in the park, it seems
      [sɪms] like an easy [izi] sport   {iF13-i:11}

(29) I've seen [sɪn] pictures of it also   {iF13-j:70}

(30) because basically it's very scenic [sɪnik]   {iF13-c:135}

Extracts 31 to 33 include three words, *if*, *cities* and *miss*, from the KIT lexical set, and the vowel in all of these has a close quality, similar to that of *means* and *easy* and not the same as *seen* and *seems*. It is possible, therefore, that there are two separate close front vowels, but that words such as *if, cities* and *miss* belong with FLEECE while *seen, seems* and *scenic* belong with KIT.

(31) yup, if [if] I'm on my own I likely won't have tried them

{iF13-c:147}

(32) the cities [sitiz] is really very crowded   {iF13c:232}

(33) will miss [mis] the teachers there lah   {iF13-g:260}

However, an alternative explanation is that FLEECE and KIT are indeed merged, but there is considerable variability in the pronunciation of the [i] vowel. This explanation is supported by the occurrence of a close vowel in the first syllable of *scenic* in extract 34, quite unlike the quality of the vowel in the same word in extract 30.

(34) basically it's because it's scenic [sinik] lah   {iF13-d:274}

Extracts 35 and 36 illustrate the merger of GOOSE and FOOT, as *food* and *cook* have a very similar vowel, and extracts 37 and 38 illustrate the merger of THOUGHT and LOT, as *taught* and *not* have a vowel with a similar quality.

(35) enjoy the food [fud] there   {iF13-c:68}

(36) you'll know how to cook [kuk]   {iF13-b:43}

(37) the instructor taught [tɔʔ] us   {iF13-i:124}

(38) I've not [nɔʔ] been there   {iF13-j:67}

2.12 DRESS and TRAP

In addition, it is often claimed that there is no distinction between the vowels in DRESS and TRAP, so *send* and *sand* generally sound the same, though Suzanna and Brown (2000) have shown that the tendency for a merger between these two vowels depends on speaking style, as educated speakers are likely to keep them distinct in formal speaking styles.

The mergers discussed above have by and large been confirmed for educated speakers by the formant measurements of Deterding (2003a), and we can attempt similar measurements for the vowels of Hui Min. A formant is a band of energy on a spectrogram, and the first two formants

Figure 2.1 Plot of the first two formants for stressed monophthongs of Hui Min.

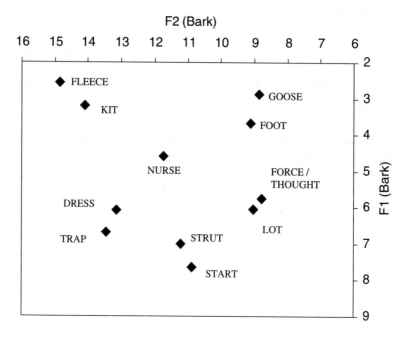

(F_1 and F_2), the two bands of energy with the lowest frequency, can easily be measured for a range of vowels using Praat software (Boersma and Weenink 2005). F_1 then gives an indication of the open/close quality of a vowel, and F_2 reflects its front/back quality. If we plot the average values of F_1 and F_2 on an auditory Bark scale, as has been done in Figure 2.1, we can obtain a representation of the open/close and also front/back quality of the vowels. In order to derive these results, the stressed vowel in an average of sixteen different words was measured for each monophthong, using the methodology described in Deterding (2003a).

Similar plots for the conversational vowels of RP British speakers (Deterding 1997) show the monophthongs fairly evenly spread around the vowel space. However, Figure 2.1 clearly shows that, for our data, the monophthongs occur in pairs. But does this mean that they are really merged?

One might conclude from Figure 2.1 that although FLEECE and KIT are quite close together, there may be a small distinction between them, and similarly for GOOSE and FOOT. However, as we have seen, if there is a distinction between FLEECE and KIT, some words such as *seen* and *seems* may unexpectedly belong with KIT, while *if* and *miss* belong with

FLEECE, and the vowel in the first syllable of *scenic* has a variable quality.

2.13 FACE and GOAT

In Singapore English, the vowels in FACE and GOAT have little change in quality during the course of the vowel, which is why we have represented them as the monophthongs [e] and [o]. Measurements of the quality of these vowels in Deterding (2000) have confirmed that there is substantially less diphthongal movement than for British English speakers, and Lee and Lim (2000) report that use of diphthongs for these vowels is perceived as 'affected' by Singaporean listeners. A monophthongal quality for these two vowels in the speech of Hui Min is illustrated for *days, own* and *know* in extracts 39 and 40.

(39) so the first few days [des] we were just wondering around on our own
[on]...yup   {iF13-c:99}

(40) friends over there who I know [no]   {iF13-a:247}

A monophthongal pronunciation of FACE and GOAT is quite common in varieties of English around the world, including those of Scotland and many speakers in America (Wells 1982: 407, 497). Deterding and Kirkpatrick (2006) have shown that it also occurs widely in the English spoken in South-East Asia.

2.14 The representation of Singapore monophthongs

Assuming a merger of vowel contrasts such as FLEECE/KIT, we can now summarise the system of eight monophthongs of Singapore English, as in Table 2.5. According to this analysis, there are three front, two central, and three back monophthongs, representing a symmetrical pattern.

However, within this simple system of eight vowels, there are some problems predicting which vowel some words have. Deterding (2005b) has shown that words such as *egg* and *bed* have a close-mid vowel, rhyming with *vague* and *made* respectively and not with *peg* and *fed*. This occurrence of [e] rather than [ɛ] in words from the DRESS lexical set tends to occur when the following consonant is voiced, but this is not entirely predictable, as both *peg* and *fed* have an open-mid vowel even though they end with a voiced consonant. It seems that the precise incidence of [e] and [ɛ] is not predictable either from the spelling or from

Table 2.5 The monophthongs of Singapore English.

	Front	Central	Back
Close	[i] (*beat, bit*)		[u] (*pool, pull*)
Close-mid	[e] (*say*)	[ə] (*heard, her*)	[o] (*know*)
Open-mid	[ɛ] (*send, sand*)		[ɔ] (*caught, cot*)
Open		[ʌ] (*cart, cut*)	

other varieties of English, though the use of [e] in both *egg* and *bed* is found consistently among nearly all Singaporeans. Deterding (2005b) argues that this demonstrates a distinct variety of English is developing in Singapore, quite independent of external varieties. In Chapter 5, we will further consider the current status of Singapore English and the extent to which it has emerged as a mature variety with its own norms of pronunciation.

Quite apart from the vowels in *egg* and *bed*, a few other words have unexpected vowels. For example, *love* sometimes has a mid central vowel [ə], not an open vowel [ʌ], especially when it is stressed and lengthened as in extract 41.

(41) I love [ləːv] them a lot   {iF13-e:284}

2.15 POOR and CURE

In Singapore, *poor, tour* and *sure* generally have a diphthong [uə], while [ɔ] occurs in words like *pure* and *cure* where the vowel follows [j] (Deterding 2005b). This is the inverse of the common pattern in modern RP British English, where [ɔː] nowadays tends to occur in *poor* and *sure*, but [ʊə] still often occurs after [j] in words such as *pure* and *cure* (Wells 2000). The use of [uə] in *tour* and *tourists* in Singapore is illustrated in extracts 42 and 43.

(42) for a tour [tuə] guide to bring you   {iF13-j:86}

(43) basically tourists [tuərists] lah, some tourists [tuərists]   {iF13-j:145}

Above, the discussion of mergers such as FLEECE/KIT and also DRESS/TRAP involves vowel distinctions that occur in British English but not in Singapore. However, with POOR, the reverse pattern is found: most young people in Britain nowadays do not make a distinction between words such as *poor* and *paw*, *tour* and *tore*, or *sure* and *shore*, but almost everyone in Singapore does distinguish them.

2.16 Triphthongs

In RP British English, the vowels in words such as *fire* and *hour* are sometimes described as triphthongs, and for many speakers, these words have just one syllable. In Singapore, these words are generally pronounced with two clear syllables, as [faijə] and [auwə] respectively (Lim and Low 2005). Extract 44 illustrates the word *require* with an inserted [j], and extracts 45 and 46 also show instances of inserted [j] in *quiet* and *retire* respectively, while extracts 47 and 48 illustrate the insertion of [w] in *hour(s)*. Deterding and Kirkpatrick (2006) have reported that a clear bisyllabic pronunciation of the triphthongs, particularly [auwə] for *our* and *hour*, is characteristic of the English spoken throughout South-East Asia.

(44)   yah which require [rikwaijə] . . . quite a lot of attention

{iF13-a:193}

(45)   it was very quiet [kwaijət], very few people were there   {iF13-j:142}

(46)   my dad has retired [ritaijəd]   {iF13-k:220}

(47)   two hours [auwəz] or less than two hours [auwəz] there

{iF13-i:107}

(48)   I guess it's about half an hour [auwə] journey   {iF13-j:169}

In Singapore, not all words that have a triphthong in RP British English necessarily have two syllables. Lim and Low (2005) have shown that while *flower* is bisyllabic as expected, *flour* is pronounced as mono-syllabic [flʌ] by nearly everyone in Singapore. Similarly, for Hui Min, *science* is monosyllabic, as seen in extract 49. Mossop (1996) also notes that *science* has [ai] in Brunei English, so maybe this pronunciation is common in the region.

(49)   English, maths and science [sains]   {iF13-h:257}

Similarly, *tuition* tends to be [tjuʃən], as in extract 50, rather than the three syllables that are found in this word in most varieties of English. Although *tuition* does not contain a triphthong (comprised of three parts, the last of which is [ə]), the simplification of the vowel in this word is perhaps rather similar to how *science* and *flour* are pronounced.

(50) stop ... I mean erm ... teaching in schools but go into tuitions
[tjuʃənz]   {iF13-h:143}

2.17 Reduced vowels

There is a tendency in Singapore English, both in monosyllabic function words and the unstressed syllables of some content words, not to use a reduced vowel (such as [ə]). In extract 51, *to* and both instances of *and* have full vowels rather than the [ə] that might be expected in many other varieties of English. However, this does not mean that [ə] never occurs, as the first syllable of *about* does have [ə].

(51) they are willing to [tu] share and [ɛn] erm tell you about [əbauʔ] teaching and [ɛn] things like that   {iF13-a:238}

Deterding (2005b) investigates the occurrence of reduced vowels in the unstressed first syllable of polysyllabic words and reports that words like *absorb* and *adventure* are likely to have a full vowel while *abroad* and *attack* are more likely to have [ə]. To make sense of this, we need to consider syllable structure. In the transcriptions shown here, we will use [.] to indicate a syllable boundary. Note that *absorb* is [ɛb.zɔb] with a closed first syllable (the vowel is followed by [b]), but *abroad* is [ə.brɔd] with an open first syllable (no consonant follows the vowel within the syllable, because the [br] constitutes the onset of the second syllable). So the conclusion is that closed syllables are more likely to have a full vowel, but many open initial syllables, especially those that are spelled with an 'a', may have [ə].

While this rule generally seems to work well, there are some exceptions. For the data of Hui Min, the pronunciation of the first vowel in polysyllabic words with an unstressed first syllable is summarised in Table 2.6, and we find that *cassette* has a full vowel whereas the rule predicts [ə], and *advised* has [ə] even though the rule predicts a full vowel. Table 2.6 also includes data for words such as *excuse* where the first syllable is spelled with 'e', and British or American English often has [ɪ] (which can also be regarded as a reduced vowel), but Singapore English often has [ɛ]. Under this category, *recorder* is an exception to the closed-syllable rule as it has [ɛ], not the predicted reduced vowel, and the rule predicts a full vowel for *exam, expensive, experience* and *extreme*, but in fact Hui Min uses a reduced vowel for all these.

Table 2.6 Realisation by Hui Min of the vowel in the unstressed first syllable of polysyllabic words.

Letter	Pronounciation	Words
'a'	full	*accessible, cassette*
	reduced	*ability, about, additional, advised, ago, another, applied, appropriate, arrange, assemble, assistant, attention, Japan, Malay, varieties*
'e'	full	*embarrassing, encounter, enjoyed, enthusiasm, environment, especially, exciting, excuse, recorder*
	reduced	*because, before, decided, degree, department, depends, Elizabeth, equipment, exam, expensive, experience, extreme, Nepal, request, retired, specific*
'o'	full	*communicate, compare, considered*
	reduced	*correct, produce, production, provide, together*
'u'	full	*subscribe, suspense*
	reduced	*support*

We should note that the absence of a reduced vowel in the unstressed first syllable of many polysyllabic words is actually also found in the North of England, and Wells (1982: 363) lists *advance, computer, consider, continue, examine, expect* and *object* (v.) as having a full vowel in their first syllable. Wells suggests that this occurs with certain prefixes of Latin origin, but we might note that all these words have a closed initial syllable. Further research is needed to determine whether the occurrence of full vowels is the same in the English of Singapore and the North of England.

In British and American English, most monosyllabic function words have two forms, a strong form that has a full vowel but only rarely occurs, and the more common weak form that usually has a reduced vowel. In Singapore, many function words only occur in their strong form, so the use of a reduced vowel in most function words is rare. However, once again this does not mean that [ə] never occurs, as *a* and *the* do usually have [ə]. In extract 52, although *but, and* and *are* all have full vowels, all four instances of *the* have [ə]. In fact, there is no hint of [ði], the strong form for *the*, even in the first token of this word which is dragged out while the speaker is pausing for thought.

(52) but [bʌʔ] then the [ðəː] . . . the [ðə] the [ðə] games and [ɛn] the [ðə] rides are [ʌ] all very expensive   {iF13-a:39}

Table 2.7 Incidence of full and reduced vowels for fifty function words in iF13-a.

Word	Full vowel	Reduced vowel
and	3	0
at	2	1
but	6	1
for	5	0
of	8	0
some	2	0
than	1	0
that	3	0
to	10	6
was	0	2
Total	40	10

To investigate the occurrence of full vowels in function words further, the pronunciation of fifty tokens of function words (ignoring those that occurred before a pause) were investigated from the first five minutes of the conversational data for Hui Min (the data in iF13-a), and the results are shown in Table 2.7. It can be seen that forty of these words (80 per cent) occur with a full vowel.

Of the ten tokens with a reduced vowel, six are instances of *to*, and further examination suggests this may partly be linked to fixed phrases, as *want to* may be pronounced as *wanna* as in extract 53, and *going to* may sometimes be *gonna* as in extract 54.

(53) initially want to [wʌnə] take the ferris wheel   {iF13-a:73}

(54) and then later on they're going to [gɔnə] have their fiftieth anniversary   {iF13-a:281}

However, even with such fixed phrases, the realisation is variable, as is illustrated by the occurrence of the full form of *to* after *want* in extract 55.

(55) first of all I want to [tu] have enough rest   {iF13-b:06}

The regular occurrence of full vowels rather than reduced vowels is not unique to Singapore. It occurs in the English found throughout South-East Asia (Deterding and Kirkpatrick 2006), in India (Kachru 2005: 46), in the English spoken in China (Deterding 2006a), and indeed in many new varieties of English such as in the Caribbean and also West Africa (Wells 1982: 570, 639).

One consequence of the relative absence of reduced vowels is the perception that the rhythm of Singapore English is syllable-based. We will now consider this.

2.18 Rhythm

The rhythm of traditional varieties of English such as those of Britain and America is often described as stress-based, as the rhythmic beat falls on the stressed syllables and there tends to be a roughly equal interval between successive stressed syllables. In contrast, in Singapore English and indeed many other new varieties of English, the rhythm is more syllable-based, as the rhythmic timing is based on individual syllables. Indeed, measurements of successive syllable durations has confirmed that there is a difference between Singapore and British English (Deterding 2001), though the most important contributory factor may be the duration of the vowel, not the whole syllable (Low et al. 2000).

Although the relative lack of reduced vowels in Singapore English is probably key to its rhythm being heard as syllable-based, there are some other important factors that also contribute to this perception, including the lack of linking between words. Furthermore, the regular occurrence of a glottal stop at the end of words plays a part in some people hearing Singapore English as having a staccato rhythm (Brown 1988a).

One problem is that all varieties of English exhibit syllable-based rhythm in certain situations (Crystal 2003: 172). Although some examples are offered here to illustrate the occurrence of syllable-based rhythm in the speech of Hui Min, it is likely that similar instances could be found in a corpus of British English data. However, even though the existence of a few examples of syllable-based rhythm does not prove anything and merely serves to illustrate the phenomenon, it probably is true that this kind of rhythm is more common in Singapore English than British or American English.

In extract 56, the last four words seem to have a very deliberate, syllable-based rhythm. We might note that the first syllable of *subscribe* has a full vowel, both instances of *to* are pronounced as [tu], and the final pronoun also has a full vowel rather than [ə], so in this example the absence of reduced vowels is indeed likely to be a significant factor in the perception of the rhythm.

(56) that is one reason why I want to subscribe to them [tu sʌbskraib tu
  dem]   {iF13-b:162}

In extract 57, the style of pronunciation is also rather deliberate, but perhaps this is just a pausing mechanism, not really syllable-based rhythm.

(57) I won't want to go back to [tu] the [ðə] city   {iF13-c:239}

In extract 58, the style is similarly quite slow, with all the syllables deliberately pronounced, maybe as a delaying tactic while the speaker is contemplating what else to say (in trying to think up something nice to say about the new campus). Extracts 59 to 61 also seem to have a syllable-based rhythm. This may be part of the linguistic repertoire of Hui Min: syllable-based rhythm is not necessarily something that characterises her speech in general, but it is a style of speaking that she uses quite regularly, to indicate certain things that she wants to place focus on or to allow herself time to think.

(58) I mean all the rooms are new   {iF13-f:68}

(59) but I was posted to Princess E   {iF13-g:219}

(60) I'm able to give them that much in three weeks ah   {iF13-a:203}

(61) because I guess I'm still a bit wary about teaching English in secondary school   {iF13-g:168}

In the previous section, it was mentioned that the relative absence of reduced vowels is something that is found in many new varieties of English throughout the world. Syllable-based rhythm is also found extensively in many emerging varieties of English, and Crystal (2003: 157) suggests that it might even become the norm for English in the future. Maybe this is one more area where Singapore is at the forefront of the development of English.

2.19 Lexical stress

One consequence of syllable-based rhythm is that it is often hard to determine which syllable within a word carries stress. In extract 62, *accessible* seems to have approximately equal stress on all four syllables. This may be a reflection of a slowing-down tactic, to allow the speaker time to think about what further to say, and, as observed above, syllable-based rhythm seems to occur quite often when someone is speaking slowly.

(62) the old campus is more accessible   {iF13-f:144}

In some words which do have a clear stress pattern, it is different from that found in other varieties of English. In extract 63, in *biographies* there is prominence on the first and last syllables, but not on the second syllable.

(63)   most likely biographies [ˈbaiɔgrʌˈfiz] of people   {iF13-f:259}

In extract 64, *opportunity* seems to have the main prominence on the second syllable, rather than the third as would be expected in British English, so we can assume that the usual stress-fixing property of the *-ity* suffix in placing the main stress on the syllable immediately before the suffix (Cruttenden 2001: 227) does not always apply in Singapore.

(64)   I just want to take the opportunity [ɔˈpɔtʃuniti] to try   {iF13-h:19}

It is often observed that *colleague* is stressed on the second syllable in Singapore (Deterding and Poedjosoedarmo 1998: 159). We have only one instance of this word in the data for Hui Min, in extract 65, and it is hard to determine where the stress falls.

(65)   other than that, erm . . . colleagues-wise I enjoy teaching
                                        {iF13-a:220}

One interesting thing to note about the pronunciation of *colleague* is that, when speakers do stress the second syllable rather than the first, this actually complies with the usual rules for lexical stress placement: a final syllable with a long vowel is generally stressed, so nouns like *machine, police, antique, mystique, esteem, typhoon, tycoon, baboon, balloon, saloon, canoe, resort, report, support, guitar, charade, facade, bazaar, return, reverse* and *concern* are all stressed on the second syllable. This means that Singaporeans who pronounce *colleague* with the stress on the second syllable are actually following the rules closely, and it is British and American speakers who break the rules, as they are more familiar with the exceptions. It seems that Singaporeans are rather good at following rules!

2.20 Sentence stress

Stress sometimes falls on unexpected words, particularly pronouns and demonstratives which would rarely be stressed in British or American English. In extract 66, there is considerable prominence on *these* even though it is not contrastive in any way.

(66)   so there's a lot of things that teachers need to be involved in . . . to
         prepare for THESE events, yup   {iF13-a:287}

Heavy emphasis also often falls on final pronouns, such as *me, them* and *him* in extracts 67 to 69.

> (67) all these are really erm . . . very new to ME . . . and erm, yup
> {iF13-c:143}

> (68) er that is one reason why I want to subscribe to THEM . . . er subscribe
> to three   {iF13-b:162}

> (69) my new nephew, he's only two months old, so I guess I will, my free
> time I'll I'll I'll . . . try to look after HIM, yah, play with HIM lah, mmm
> {iF13-b:193}

Prominence on a final pronoun in Singapore English is similarly reported by Levis (2005), and it is common in the English found throughout South-East Asia (Deterding and Kirkpatrick 2006) and also the English of speakers from China (Deterding 2006a).

2.21 Deaccenting

In British or American English, content words which are repeated are not usually given prominence, a process known as deaccenting. However, it has been shown that this kind of deaccenting often does not take place in Singapore (Deterding 1994; Levis 2005). In extract 70, although *library* is repeated, it is not deaccented, even though one might expect *old* to be the key information in the second clause as the old library is being contrasted with the library on the new campus.

> (70) I guess I like the library the most . . . yah . . . it it's it really is erm very
> different from the old LIBRARY . . . yup   {iF13-f:10}

As with stress on final pronouns discussed in the previous section, we might note that *library* in extract 70 is the final word (apart from the pause particle *yup*), so it is possible that the intonation pattern here is being used to indicate the end of the utterance.

Similarly in extract 71, although *cook* is repeated, its second occurrence receives substantial prominence.

> (71) but erm other than that, I would love to learn to . . . to cook, yah,
> because basically I don't know how to COOK   {iF13-b:23}

Goh (2005) notes that the assignment of prominence to a final word regardless of whether it carries new information or not is a feature of

Singapore English, and this suggests that it fulfils an important function, to mark the end of the utterance. One conclusion drawn by Goh is that a model of discourse intonation established for British English needs some modifications before it can be applied to the analysis of English in Singapore.

2.22 Early booster

There is a tendency for prominent high pitch to occur at the start of an utterance in Singapore, something that has been termed 'boosted pitch' (Deterding 1994) and an early 'booster' (Low 2000). This can be illustrated by the pitch found on *actually* and *basically*. These words occur about as often as in British English, but they become especially salient in Singapore partly because they tend to occur early in the utterance, in contrast with their quite common occurrence in final position in British English, and especially because of the sharply rising pitch they often carry in Singapore (Doyle and Deterding 2005). This substantial rise in pitch over the course of the word is shown using the symbol '↑' in the middle of the words *actually* and *basically* in extracts 72 to 75. The use of *actually* and *basically* will be discussed further in Chapter 4 on discourse.

(72) and act↑ually I would like to visit there one day   {iF13-j:72}

(73) basi↑cally it's a good combination ah   {iF13-a:172}

(74) maths basi↑cally is about doing tutorials   {iF13-g:54}

(75) so basi↑cally most of my family members stay around ... us stay around me lah   {iF13-k:172}

The occurrence of an early booster is not restricted to *actually* and *basically*, as it also occurs in phrases such as *I think* and *I guess*, as illustrated in extracts 76 to 79.

(76) I ↑ think they are quite ... nice and interesting magazines
{iF13-b:173}

(77) I ↑ think one place that I can compare with Switzerland easily is New Zealand   {iF13-d:276}

(78) so I ↑ guess I will try to go to the park to cycle   {iF13-b:97}

(79) I ↑ guess the most recent trip will be to ... to Japan   {iF13-c:218}

In fact, although *actually, basically, I think* and *I guess* seem to be especially common carriers of this early booster, it can occur on any word, as illustrated by its occurrence on *trip* in extract 80 and *before* in 81.

> (80) er the ↑ trip to Sydney was . . . erm only for a few days with a group of friends   {iF13-d:11}

> (81) but be↑fore I was retrenched I actually applied for teaching already   {iF13-e:166}

This use of an early booster illustrates one way in which the intonation of Singapore English is quite distinct from that of British English, and it demonstrates once again how a framework designed for the description of intonation in British or American English may not be appropriate for Singapore.

2.23 Rising tone

The early booster mentioned in the previous section occurs near the start of an utterance. Quite distinct from that is a high-rising pitch movement at the end of an utterance. Sometimes, this can easily be explained, as the utterance is part of a list and the rising tone indicates a non-final item. This is illustrated by the rising pitch (shown by '↗') on *low* in extract 82, where the speaker is giving a list of reasons why she was advised not to accept a job in a library. Such use of a rising tone to indicate the non-final item of a list is common in most varieties of English.

> (82) one thing the pay will be very ↗low . . . another thing you'll be doing something very simple   {iF13-e:223}

However, at other times it is hard to identify any kind of list for the rising intonation at the end of an utterance. In extract 83, the rising tone on *varieties* maybe indicates uncertainty. It is almost like a question, though it does not seem as if the speaker is actually expecting an answer.

> (83) then er, English movies I guess more ↗varieties . . . maybe, yah, then what kind of movies, ah   (iF13-b:238)

A similar instance of rising intonation that seems to be asking a question is extract 84. One possibility is that the rise on *funfair* is indeed a kind of question, checking whether the listener is familiar with the funfair at

Jurong East. Another possibility is that it is indicating that this is a topic the speaker intends to continue talking about for a while.

> (84) then later on in the evening . . . er went to the UK ⁄funfair . . . at Jurong
>   East   (iF13-a:30)

In extract 85, the rising intonation on *nephews* seems to indicate that the speaker intended to continue, but then there is falling intonation on *yup* (shown by 'ᵥ'), so in fact it is not entirely clear what the purpose of the rising intonation on *nephews* indicates. Maybe the speaker changed her mind and then said *yup* to conclude that part of the utterance. The very regular occurrence of *yup*, sometimes to indicate some kind of completion, will be discussed further in Chapter 4 on discourse.

> (85) play with my niece and ⁄nephews . . . ᵥyup . . . bring them out . . . to the
>   library   {iF13-b:111}

It has sometimes been claimed that all questions in Singapore English have a rising tone, including wh-questions which more often have a falling tone in other varieties of English (Tay 1982). However, little actual evidence for this has ever been presented in the literature. Although there are few questions in our data for Hui Min, extract 86 does include a wh-question, and there is clearly a falling intonational contour at the end of this utterance.

> (86) mmm what else do I do during the free ᵥtime   {iF13-b:125}

2.24 Rise-fall tone

A rise-fall tone is used quite often in Singapore English to indicate an extra degree of emphasis. This pattern is quite distinct from the use of a rise-fall tone in British English, often to indicate something suggestive. In extract 87, the rise-fall tone (indicated by '^') occurs on the word *cycle*, though it is not immediately clear if there is really an extra degree of emphasis intended on this word. In extract 88, a rise-fall tone occurs on *crowded*, and in extract 89, it occurs on *attention*.

> (87) so I guess I will try to go to the park to ^cycle   {iF13-b:97}
>
> (88) then I can go earlier, then it'll be, it won't be so ^crowded
>   {iF13-b:101}
>
> (89) which require . . . quite a lot of ^attention   {iF13-a:194}

2.25 Final lengthening

There is a tendency for the final syllable of an utterance to be dragged out, as in extract 90, where the end of *fifty* gets lengthened before the pause, and similarly for *countries* in extract 91 and *anniversary* in extract 92.

(90) then about seven fifty [fifti:] . . . wah   {iF13-a:65}

(91) erm I have been to quite a few countries [kʌntri:z]   {iF13-c:04}

(92) and then later on they're going to have their fiftieth anniversary [ɛnivəsəri:] . . . er celebration   {iF13-a:281}

This final lengthening seems similar to a pattern that occurs quite regularly in Malay. We will now consider where the distinctive intonational patterns of Singapore English come from.

2.26 Influences on Singapore intonation

Some analysts assume that, because the overwhelming majority of Singaporeans are ethnically Chinese, the major substrate language must be a variety of Chinese, either Mandarin or one of the regional dialects such as Hokkien or Cantonese (Ho and Platt 1993; Bao 2001). However, this overlooks two things: first, Singapore has always had close links with Malaysia, where the majority of the people are not Chinese, and indeed, until recently the English of Singapore was generally assumed to be closely linked to that of Malaysia (Lim 2001); and second, historically many ethnically Chinese people in Singapore spoke a variety of Malay rather than any variety of Chinese, so it is quite likely that their speech was affected more by Malay than Chinese.

Chinese is a tone language, so each morpheme has a fixed tone that cannot be changed according to the intonation, but there is little evidence of fixed tonal movements in the intonational patterns discussed here (apart, perhaps, from the regular use of an early booster on *actually* and *basically*). In fact, some patterns, particularly the rise-fall tone and final lengthening, seem to originate more from Malay than from Chinese.

The suggestion that Malay may be the origin of much of the distinctive intonation of Singapore English overlooks one important fact that was alluded to in Chapter 1: Singaporeans can easily detect the ethnic background of a local speaker on the basis of just a few seconds of English speech, and this ability seems to be based mostly on intonation, so it seems that the intonation of the English of Singaporean Malays is very different from that of Singaporean Chinese. One might surmise, therefore, that although the intonation of the English of all Singaporeans may be influenced by Malay, the extent of this influence varies between the different ethnic groups.

3 Morphology and Syntax

Morphology deals with how words are constructed, including the use of affixes. There seems little difference from other varieties of English in the ways derivational suffixes such as *-ity, -ness, -ology* and *-ism* are used in Singapore. Occasionally one finds them attached to borrowed words, such as *kiasuism* meaning 'the act of being *kiasu*' (where *kiasu* is borrowed from Hokkien and means 'fear of losing out'), and the somewhat jokey *chimology* meaning 'the study of being *chim*' (where *chim* is a borrowed word meaning 'profound'). Extracts 1 and 2 illustrate the use of these two words in blogs.

(1) So I should give more inputs to enhance my employability. Am I too 'kiasu'? Maybe. Kiasuism is the production of the competition, I suppose.   {Vicky, 8/6/06}

(2) they discussed the topic on 'occult'. Man! It's *chimology*.

{SK, 7/5/06}

The creation of new words such as these indicates that derivational suffixes are productive and that Singaporeans manipulate them in the same way as other users of English.

There is somewhat more difference in the ways inflectional suffixes occur in Singapore English when compared to the usage found in traditional varieties of English such as those of Britain or America. Here, we will consider inflectional suffixes such as *-ed* in the past-tense form of the verb and *-s* in both the third-person singular present-tense form of the verb and the plural form of the noun.

In this chapter, we will also discuss other syntactic issues such as the occurrence of the modal verbs *will* and *would*, the occasional omission of the copula verb *be*, the use of the perfective, the meaning of *till*, relative pronouns, reduplication of words, invariant utterance-final tags, the incidence of extra prepositions, and finally the occurrence of null-subject structures.

3.1 Analysis of inflectional suffixes

One problem in the analysis of the past-tense -*ed* suffix is that it is usually pronounced as [t] or [d], and as was discussed in Chapter 2, final [t] and [d] are often omitted in Singapore English especially when they occur after another consonant, and in fact this also occurs quite regularly in RP British English broadcast by the BBC even when the [t] or [d] represents an -*ed* suffix (Deterding 2006b). As a result, in an example such as extract 3 where Hui Min is narrating a story about her past attempts to learn to swim, we cannot be certain if *kick, move* and *stop* are instances of present-tense forms of the verb or if in fact they are past-tense forms with the final sound omitted because of consonant cluster simplification. In other words, we cannot tell if the absence of the final [t] and [d] in these words is a morphosyntactic process or a phonological process.

(3) when I kick(ed) [kik] my hands doesn't move, when I when I move(d) [muv] my hands, my my feet stop(ped) [stɔp] kicking   {iF13-i:155}

In this extract, there might be a temptation to regard all the verbs as present-tense forms on the basis that *doesn't* is clearly in the present tense, but in fact we have no evidence for the other three verbs, and we need to acknowledge that in all three cases, especially as the next word begins with a consonant, [kik], [muv] and [stɔp] actually represent a perfectly normal pronunciation of the past-tense forms with omission of the final sound due to consonant cluster simplification. Therefore, although Ho and Platt (1993) provide detailed figures for the occurrence of present and past-tense forms of verbs – reporting, for example, that in their data only 56.2 per cent of punctual verbs are marked for past tense where prescriptively such marking is expected (1993: 86) – we will not attempt to provide such precise numbers for tense marking in the data considered here.

In contrast, for the -*s* suffix, detailed figures can be provided, because there is no phonological process leading to the omission of final [s] and [z] in the variety of educated Singapore English represented by the speech of Hui Min. This can be demonstrated by considering all instances of words with a final consonant cluster ending with [s] where this sound is not a suffix. In the data for Hui Min, we find *else, experience, science, substance, suspense, six, sense, influence, once* and *chance*, many of which occur a number of times in the recording, and there is not one instance of omission of the final consonant. All of these involve final [s] and none of them have [z], as words with non-suffix [z] at the end of a word-final consonant cluster (such as in *lens* or *bronze*) are quite rare in English, but it seems reasonable to assume that, for this speaker, the absence of a phonological process deleting final [s] extends to [z] as well. As a result, we can be confident that any omission of a final [s] or [z] is a morphological issue and not a phonological instance of consonant cluster simplification.

3.2 Plural marking on nouns

It is sometimes claimed that a distinction between count and non-count nouns is not maintained in Singapore English, but it would be more accurate to say that a few nouns such as *furniture* and *lighting* which are non-count in other varieties of English are treated as count in Singapore. In many ways, therefore, Singapore adopts a rather logical approach to the classification of nouns, as both *furniture* and *lighting* refer to things which might quite reasonably be viewed as countable. The use of *furniture* as a count noun in the NIECSSE data is illustrated in extract 4, while the use of *furniture* and *lighting* as count nouns in blogs is shown in extracts 5 and 6.

(4)   so I bought a lot of erm furnitures from IKEA

{NIECSSE, F10-e:24}

(5)   Going to IKEA to look for a few furnitures for my bro's room and some paints.   {Anikin Goh, 4/1/06}

(6)   my Dad brought me to Balestier to buy lightings for the new house.

{Ryan, 4/6/06}

Similarly, in extracts 7 and 8 we find *stuff* being used as a count noun, and extract 9 includes the use of a plural form for *clothing.*

(7)   I won't have time . . . to erm do any research . . . stuffs like that

{NIECSSE, F24-c:29}

(8)   might get another camera body from the seller again. Great guy lah, super friendly. And his stuffs are SUPER cheap.

{Timothy Tan, 26/11/05}

(9)   I had to borrow some . . . winter clothings from er . . . my husband's erm . . . boss I think he was the boss   {NIECSSE, F17-b:15}

The data from Hui Min also has various instances of logically countable things being treated as count nouns. In extract 10, *fiction* is used as a count noun (just as *novel* is count in most varieties of English). Similarly, one might argue that it is perfectly logical to treat *company* as count as in extract 11, seeing as it involves a number of friends, and possibly also *tuition* in extract 12, as it entails multiple visits to the homes of different pupils.

(10) and reading some fictions [fikʃəmps]   {iF13-b:70}

(11) yah, then quite a few of my friends are in here also . . . doing their Honours . . . yah, so I mean there are, there are companies ah . . . I have companies with me so I guess . . . er won't be so lonely   {iF13-h:51}

(12) will I want to stop . . . I mean erm . . . teaching in schools but go into tuitions . . . or or . . . private teaching or what I don't know
                                                              {iF13-h:141}

It is important to note that Hui Min does use some non-count nouns, as illustrated by *experience* in extract 13, *support* in 14, *money* in 15, and *income* in 16, so the distinction between count and non-count is mostly present (with some exceptions discussed below). It is just that some nouns, including *fiction, company* and *tuition,* have been reanalysed as count as they seem logically countable in many circumstances.

(13) three weeks experience   {iF13-a:166}

(14) the class would be able to provide more support . . . for these children
                                                              {iF13-a:212}

(15) I will waste my money ((laughs))   {iF13-b:263}

(16) these two years I've not . . . been travelling much because er no income
                                                              {iF13-c:10}

There are, however, a few cases where the occurrence of an -*s* suffix on nouns is more unexpected, as occasionally it is omitted when the noun refers to a plural entity or is added for a singular noun. In extract 17, Hui Min uses an -*s* suffix on the second instance of *weekend* even though she is quite clearly talking only about the previous weekend and has just uttered the word without an -*s* suffix, and in extract 18, she says *brothers* even though she in fact has only one brother.

(17) last weekend, erm I went to . . . I did quite a few things during the weekends . . . firstly I went back to the primary school that I taught for the last three weeks   {iF13-a:03}

(18) when erm . . . all of us, as in myself and my sisters and brothers er were studying   {iF13-l:18}

For omission of an expected plural suffix, we find *country* in extract 19, even though lots of countries are actually listed.

(19)   I mean the few country that I've been to are ... erm ... Australia ... Bali ... erm Turkey ... er Hong Kong ... Taiwan ... Korea, Japan, Nepal ... er ... yah, I think basically that   {iF13-c:23}

Alsagoff and Ho (1998: 144) state that the plural suffix always occurs with a premodifying quantifier such as *four* or *many*. However, *few* is also a premodifying quantifier, so extract 19 seems to provide evidence against their claim. Wee and Ansaldo (2004: 64) also question whether plural nouns always occur after quantifiers in Singapore English, offering 'ten thousand of my friend' from their data as a counter-example.

Despite these instances of unexpected added or omitted plural -*s* suffixes, the overwhelming majority of nouns have the standard plural marking. For example, Hui Min says 'my niece and nephews' consistently, and it turns out that she does indeed have one niece and two nephews. In extract 20 she refers to 'my niece and nephew', with no plural suffix on *nephew*, but in fact as her younger nephew is still a baby who does not yet go to school, the omission of an -*s* suffix on *nephew* is an accurate reflection of the fact that, in this case, she is referring to just one nephew.

(20)   so that it's easier for my niece and nephew to go to s- to a nearby school ... um, in our area   {iF13-k:63}

3.3 Third-person singular marking on verbs

Occasionally, use of the -*s* suffix on present-tense verbs is variable. Sometimes it does not occur as expected when the subject is third-person singular, and at other times an unexpected suffix appears. In extract 21, an -*s* suffix occurs even after the modal verb *will* when one would expect the base form of the verb (with no suffix) instead.

(21)   my mum will always says that never mind lah, next time when you get married, you'll know how to cook   {iF13-b:40}

However, the extent of this variability should not be exaggerated for the variety of educated Singapore English investigated here, as in the speech of Hui Min the overwhelming majority of present-tense verbs are marked as they would be in British or American English. In fact, there are a total of 156 present-tense verbs with a third-person subject, and the

Table 3.1 Form of present-tense verbs with third-person subject for Hui Min.

	-s form	no -s
3rd singular subject	109	9
3rd plural subject	3	35

occurrence of an -*s* form for these verbs is summarised in Table 3.1, showing that twelve verbs have an unexpected form of the verb, three having -*s* even though the subject is plural and nine with no -*s* after a singular subject. Furthermore, with first-person subjects (*I* and *we*), there are no unexpected uses of the -*s* form of the verb.

The three instances of the -*s* form of the verb with a plural subject are shown in extracts 22 to 24.

(22) the the cities is really very crowded   {iF13-c:232}

(23) when I kick(ed), my hands doesn't move   {iF13-i:155}

(24) I like places that is quiet lah   {iF13-j:223}

One of the instances of the absence of the -*s* form of the verb is *have* in extract 25, which might be analysed as *everyone* being treated as a plural noun. Alternatively, one might say the -*s* suffix has turned up (twice!) rather unexpectedly on the end of *been*.

(25) I mean everyone have beens talk- have beens ... talking about it, whether you'll be posted to a secondary school or JC   {iF13-g:134}

A few of the other instances of missing -*s* suffixes with singular subjects are *require* in extract 26, *do* in 27 and *look* in 28.

(26) and that require you to be able ... you yourself be enthusiastic about the subject   {iF13-h:287}

(27) other than that, he ... he do some ... er ... pen-zai ah, bonsai ah, you call that, yah   {iF13-k:259}

(28) nowadays she ... she look after my niece and nephews, yah
          {iF13-l:09}

Given this rate of over 92 per cent for the expected subject-verb agreement with third-person subjects, it is best to conclude that this agreement is standard with just a few exceptions rather than suggest that use of the -*s* suffix is random.

3.4 Tenses

Much work has been done quantifying the occurrence of past-tense forms, especially by Ho and Platt (1993). However, as discussed above, there is a problem about whether to classify the omission of final [t] and [d] as a phonological or syntactic process, so no attempt will be made here to provide detailed figures for past-tense usage.

Although it is often not possible to be certain about the tense usage with regular verbs, many irregular verbs do offer reliable analysis, as the past-tense form of some irregular verbs involves a change in the vowel or some other salient difference in the pronunciation. On the basis of tense usage for irregular verbs, we find that, even when clearly narrating a story, Hui Min often starts with the past tense but then slips into the present tense, as in extract 29.

> (29) then later on in the evening . . . er went to the UK funfair . . . at Jurong East . . . mmm . . . it was, it was interesting, but very expensive . . . erm the fun, the entrance fee is cheap, it's only two dollars . . . I guess that's cheap enough, but then the . . . the games and the rides are all very expensive {iF13-a:30}

One possible explanation for this occurrence of tenses is that the present tense is used to refer to something that is still true (Deterding 2003b). In extract 29 Hui Min uses *went* for an action and *was* for her impressions during the event, but then if we assume that the funfair was still running when she was talking about it, we can propose a logical explanation for her use of *is* and *are* to refer to things that continued to be true at the time of her conversation.

However, this interpretation for the use of present tense in narratives does not explain all instances. In extract 30, the speaker is talking about her experience teaching in a primary school, and although all of the events occurred in the past, after using the past tense *didn't* at the start, she slips into use of the present tense for the rest of the extract.

> (30) so didn't really enjoy the three weeks there ((laughs)) I guess it's because I know that I'm only be there for three weeks . . . and um . . . yah so um . . . mmm . . . er . . . so don't know whether to um . . . to put all my heart in there {iF13-a:137}

In fact, the tendency to switch into the present tense when narrating a past event seems characteristic of much of Hui Min's speech. In extract 31, she is talking about the kind of work she did during a previous job in a factory which has now closed down. Even though there is no possibility that the situation is still true, she uses the present tense throughout this extract.

(31) there are times when you are very busy, and there are times when there's erm . . . mmm mmm . . . not as busy lah, yah, so er the busy time will be when there's there are many new models, yah, so you have to test them out, on the line when the production is not running

{iF13-e:110}

One other feature of extract 31 is the use of *will* even when talking about a past event. We will consider the use of *will* in Singapore English in the next section.

Ho and Platt (1993: 86) suggest that use of the present tense for past events is most common for non-punctual verbs, which includes stative verbs that depict a situation and also verbs describing a habitual action, and indeed it is true that in the previous examples many of the unexpected uses of the present tense involve non-punctual verbs.

In conclusion, it seems that use of past-tense forms of verbs is quite variable, even when narrating a story, and there is a pattern of slipping into the present tense as soon as the past time of the events has been established, especially for stative verbs and those describing something habitual. This variable use of tense contrasts with the largely consistent use of the -*s* suffix on present-tense verbs to achieve agreement with a third-person singular subject. One explanation for this is that the -*s* suffix is perceptually quite salient, while in contrast the past-tense suffix can often be dropped without anyone noticing, especially for regular verbs with a final [t] or [d], and this flexibility in the use of the regular past-tense suffix might extend to cases of irregular verbs as well. An alternative explanation might be that, once the time frame of an event has clearly been established, use of the past tense is largely redundant, so speakers see no need to keep on repeating this information. In contrast, the -*s* third-person suffix always has a role, as it helps to confirm the identity of the subject for each clause, and as it thereby contributes to establishing the structure of the sentence, it is never truly redundant. It is hard to determine which of these two explanations – perceptual saliency or grammatical redundancy – is more important in the different treatment of subject-verb agreement and past-tense usage.

3.5 *Will*

It is usual in most varieties of English for *will* to refer to future events. Though it can also occasionally be used for prediction about current things ('That will be the postman' on hearing a knock at the door), such usage is rare. In contrast, in Singapore *will* is often used for regular events, such as in extract 32 where Hui Min is saying that she often reads magazines which her sisters buy.

> (32) basically my sisters, they will buy . . . magazines like Her World, Cleo,
> er female magazines, yah, then I will just um . . . take the opportunity
> to to read them lah   {iF13-b:140}

In extract 33, Hui Min is talking about her mother's reaction to her repeated failure to learn to cook, and even though *every time* serves to signal the regularity of this event explicitly, *will* is used. Similarly, *will* occurs in extract 34 to describe her grandmother's frequent visits, and in 35 it is used to refer to the daily ferry trips to two of the tiny islands just to the south of the main island of Singapore.

> (33) I have wanted to do that . . . for quite some time already, but every time
> during the holidays, I'm too lazy to . . . to do it, and then my m- my
> mum will always says that never mind lah, next time when you get
> married, you'll know how to cook   {iF13-b:33}

> (34) at times my grandmother will come over to our place   {iF13-k:160}

> (35) actually the ferry will fetch people to Kusu Island and then to St John
> Island   {iF13-j:265}

In fact, the tendency to use *will* to refer to regular events extends to things that occurred in the past, as mentioned above for extract 31. In extract 36, the past nature of the event is signalled by the use of *last time*, and in extract 37, she is talking about a previous trip to Australia, but *will* occurs in both extracts.

> (36) last time, erm . . . she will um babysit for other people   {iF13-l:13}

> (37) er the trip to Sydney was . . . um only for a few days with a group of
> friends . . . yah actually we were there for some . . . church ac- activity,
> basically, but other than that we will go sightseeing   {iF13-d:10}

Overall, disregarding repetitions and also excluding reduced forms such as *I'll* (for which it is hard to be certain of the existence of the *'ll* clitic, especially given the frequency of dark [l] vocalisation as discussed in Chapter 2), there are seventy-three clear instances of *will* in the one hour of data for Hui Min, and only nineteen of these actually refer to future time.

The use of *will* for a regular event is not just an idiosyncrasy of the speech of Hui Min, as it has been observed for a wide range of different speakers in Singapore (Deterding 2003b). For example, from the NIECSSE data, we find extracts 38 (from a Malay Singaporean), and extracts 39 and 40 (both from Chinese Singaporeans), and in all of these *will* refers to a regular event.

(38) at night we will . . . most of us will go to . . . mosque . . . and . . . we have
to pray   {NIECSSE, F4-c:07}

(39) I do studying like after dinner after watching some TV shows and . . .
after talking to friends, then I will start studying
{NIECSSE, F19-f:38}

(40) it's about . . . one hour and forty-five minutes . . . so to and fro you will
chalk up about four hours   {NIECSSE, F20-e:05}

One possible source for this use of *will* in describing a habitual event is the Chinese auxiliary verb *hui* (会). Although *hui* usually signals ability ('know how to') or future time (Li and Thompson 1981: 183), it can also occur in sentences describing a repeated action, as in the following example:

wo	zai	cai-shi-chang	de	shi-hou	hui	shuo	hua-yu
I	at	vegetable-market	NOM	time	will	speak	Chinese-language

'Whenever I am at the market, I speak Chinese.'

However, given the fact that Mandarin has only recently become a widely spoken language in Singapore, perhaps we should be looking at other varieties of Chinese for influences on Singapore English. In Hokkien, the auxiliary verb *bhe* (equivalent to Mandarin *yao* 要) is very common to indicate both future and regular events, and its use for a regular event is illustrated in the following sentence from an introduction to Taiwanese Hokkien (Taiwan Language Committee 2005: 15). Perhaps this is the source of *will* for regular events in Singapore English.

na	si	gi-ta^n	e	si-gan	bhe	an zua^n	gong
if	is	other	NOM	time	will	how	say

'What do you say at other times?'

3.6 *Would*

In British and other varieties of English, there is a grammatical distinction between a possible conditional ('I will go to the shops if I have time') and a hypothetical conditional describing an imaginary situation ('I would go to the shops if I had time'), and *would* usually occurs in the main clause of the latter. In Singapore, the grammatical category of hypothetical conditional does not generally exist. For example, at the end of extract 41, the speaker uses *won't* rather than *wouldn't* even though she is discussing what might have happened if she had been on her own and that is a purely imaginary situation.

> (41) the other trip I liked . . . was to Nepal, yah, because basically it's very scenic, yah and then the trekking, the rafting, all these and then, and the safari that we visit, all these are really erm very new to me, and erm . . . yup, if I'm on my own I likely won't have tried them, yah
> {iF13-c:131}

Instead of occurring in hypothetical conditionals, *would* is often used in Singapore to indicate that something is tentative (Deterding 2003b). In extract 42, Hui Min is discussing her plans to learn to swim, and this is a possible event though she is a little hesitant about it. As she has just been talking about an instance when she almost drowned when trying to learn to swim, she is probably not particularly keen to try it again, so it is not surprising if she harbours a certain degree of apprehension towards swimming.

> (42) so if I can, I would hope to learn swimming   {iF13-i:60}

In extract 43, maybe she is a little unsure whether her choice to focus on English rather than maths was right, so the use of *would* reflects this uncertainty.

> (43) if I'm going to teach in a primary school I feel that maybe English would be more appropriate . . . to . . . major in than maths
> {iF13-g:103}

In extract 44, she is talking about whether she will go back to the same school that she did her teaching practice in, and the fact that she corrects herself is significant. Initially, she starts to say that she *won't* ask to go back there, but then she amends this and uses *would not* instead, to emphasise that she has not yet decided.

(44) seriously, I I guess I don't know, now . . . at the moment, I feel that I
won't want, I mmm likelihood I would not request . . . to go back
{iF13-g:206}

The use of *would* to indicate tentativeness is frequent in the
NIECSSE data as well. In extract 45, the speaker uses *would* to indicate
that she is not certain if the knowledge will actually be useful, and in
extract 46 the speaker becomes a bit confused about how old each of her
four children is, so she uses *would* to reflect her uncertainty at that point,
but then she amends it to *she's* when she is more confident that she has
sorted it all out.

(45) I feel that the knowledge would help {NIECSSE, F24-d:45}

(46) my eldest is eleven . . . erm number th- three . . . sorry number two
would be, she's six now {NIECSSE, F15-b:01}

Sometimes *would* is just used as a variant of *will* to refer to a regular
event, though perhaps it still indicates a degree of tentativeness. In
extract 47, also from the NIECSSE data, the student pauses after saying
would, probably reflecting some hesitation on her part in claiming that
she studies so diligently in school every day.

(47) I usually would . . . study in school until the evenings
{NIECSSE, F14-h:04}

Overall, in the one hour of speech by Hui Min, *would* is used nineteen
times (though, to be honest, there are some cases where one cannot be
absolutely sure if *would* or *will* is used), so it is rather less frequent than
the seventy-three instances of *will*.

3.7 Absence of *be*

Many observers have commented on the tendency for the copula verb *be*
to be omitted in Singapore English. Ho and Platt (1993: 31) give the
example 'I damn naughty', and they report that *be* actually gets omitted
in about 13 per cent of potential cases. However, this omission of the
copula is more frequent in colloquial varieties of the language than the
educated variety being considered here, and indeed Gupta (1994: 11)
lists BE-deletion as one diagnostic for the use of colloquial Singapore
English. In the data of Hui Min, two instances that can be analysed as
having no verb are extracts 48 and 49, though in the first of these the

missing verb might be *have* rather than some form of the copula, or maybe *English movies* is the topic, and both the subject and the verb (*there + are*) are omitted.

(48)   English movies I guess more varieties   {iF13-b:238}

(49)   the younger ones . . . all all right also lah   {iF13-a:242}

In his analysis of the speech of Hui Min, Tan (2007) similarly regards extract 49 as having topic prominence, partly because of the pause after *ones*, and on this analysis the utterance has a null subject as well as a missing verb. Instances of a null subject together with a missing verb are quite common in the speech of Hui Min, but this results in stand-alone noun phrases and other sentence fragments which are frequent in all varieties of spoken English, so we will not examine them here. Null subjects are discussed later in this chapter, and topic prominence is considered in Chapter 4.

3.8 Perfective

In Singapore, there is a tendency to use *already* instead of the *have* (or *had*) auxiliary to indicate perfective aspect, as illustrated in extracts 50 and 51.

(50)   and I have . . . three other sisters and a youngest brother, yup, so um, all of us already, I mean . . . except myself, the rest of them already um . . . um completed their studying   {iF13-k:21}

(51)   but before I was retrenched I actually applied for teaching already
                                                                      {iF13-e:166}

A similar example of *already* to indicate perfective aspect is found in the NIECSSE data in extract 52. In an example such as this, in British or American English one might instead find 'he's been with Ericsson'.

(52)   but he's with Ericsson for . . . about . . . I think eight years already
                                                                {NIECSSE, F17-d:22}

Bao (1995) has noted that there are in fact two distinct meanings for *already* in Singapore English: it can indicate completion as in extracts 50 and 51 above, but it can also sometimes carry an inchoative meaning, indicating that something has just started to occur. Bao (1995: 1ᵒ³) gives the example 'My baby speak already', where standard

English might use 'My baby has started to speak', and he argues that the Singapore use of *already* is derived from the Mandarin *le* (了) particle.

3.9 *Until* and *till*

In British English, *until* and *till* indicate that something stops being true at the time mentioned, so 'They talked until midnight' means the conversation stopped at twelve o'clock, and 'I never understood it till now' means that the state of confusion has now ceased. In Singapore, *until* and *till* may be used to indicate that something continues to be true beyond the stated time. Bao and Wee (1998) argue that the Singapore usage is influenced by the Mandarin Chinese word *dao* (到) and they give the following example sentence of something continuing up to and beyond the specified time (p. 37).

tamen	tan	dao	ban ye,	hai	zai	tan
they	talk	DAO	half night	still	PROG	talk

'they talked until midnight, and were still talking'

This meaning for *till* is sometimes found in the data for Hui Min. In extract 53, the lack of confidence in teaching extends into the present time; in extract 54, she still has not managed to learn to swim; and in extract 55, the baby continues to be good.

(53) because . . . till now I still feel that I lack the ability to teach well
{iF13-h:168}

(54) so till now still don't know how to swim   {iF13-i:204}

(55) till now the baby is still not so bad lah   {iF13-l:142}

However, note that all these three extracts involve the phrase *till now* and also include the word *still*, so perhaps these three words tend to occur together for Hui Min, as a kind of three-word collocation. In fact, she sometimes does use *till* to indicate that the event stopped at the stated time, as illustrated by extract 56 where her research did not continue beyond three-thirty.

(56) after that I came back to NIE to do . . . some library research . . . till about three-thirty   {iF13-a:22}

3.10 Relative pronouns

There is a widespread belief among speakers of English in Singapore that, for a relative pronoun with a human antecedent, use of *that* is ungrammatical and only *who* or *whom* can be used (Newbrook 2003), even though *that* is in fact very common in this context in other varieties of English. In both extracts 57 and 58, the relative pronoun is *who*.

> (57) so hopefully the teacher who took over . . . the class will be able to provide more support   {iF13-a:207}

> (58) I will talk to a few of my friends who are already posted out . . . teaching in schools   {iF13-g:280}

Of course, the use of *who* in these two extracts is also possible in British or American English, but *that* might also occur in both of these utterances.

In fact, in the data for Hui Min, there is one instance where *that* does occur with a human antecedent, in extract 59, so perhaps the non-human restriction on its use in Singapore applies mostly to written language.

> (59) so, erm nowadays some of the kids that she have brought up, actually do keep in tou- contact with her, yah   {iF13-l:38}

Alsagoff (1995) also notes the use of *one* as a relative pronoun, though it occurs at the end of the relative clause rather than at the start as expected in standard English, and she gives the example 'That boy pinch my sister one very naughty' (1995: 85). This occurs only in colloquial Singapore English, not the educated variety exemplified by Hui Min, so we have no examples here of *one* being used as a relative pronoun. It would be interesting to offer some examples of this usage from blogs, but it is not straightforward to search for *one* occurring as a relative pronoun with the web-based tools currently available, so no clear instances were found.

3.11 Reduplication

Many descriptions of the syntax of Singapore English discuss reduplication of words in some detail. For example, Wee (2004c) lists *cry-cry* to indicate crying a little bit, while reduplication of a noun such as *boy-boy* shows intimacy.

For the data of Hui Min, most of the instances of word repetition involve stuttering or hesitation, and these are entirely different from the kind of reduplication discussed by Wee. Similarly, in the NIECSSE data there are no instances of non-stuttering word reduplication, as this phenomenon seems to belong more within the realm of colloquial Singapore English. For data on doubled words, we therefore turn to blogs, where we find the following instances. In extract 60, *walk walk* indicates going for a stroll, while in extract 61, *buddy buddy* probably indicates intimacy.

(60) Then as YukLum suggested we went to Singapore River to walk walk.

{Jing, 5/5/06}

(61) Im the kind who is buddy buddy person   {Defy Angel, 16/6/06}

Sometimes, the reduplication involves three instances of a word or phrase, and in extract 62, from the data of Hui Min, we do find one instance of this kind of repetition of *a bit*, probably to indicate the frequency of doing the sports. (The fourth instance of *a bit* is after a pause and is not part of this kind of systematic reduplication.)

(62) all these torp- sports I did a bit a bit a bit . . . of a bit of them during um . . . um um previously ah   {iF13-i:247}

According to Wee (2004c), three repetitions such as this usually occur with a verb and indicate continuity. In extract 63 from a blog, *wait wait wait* expresses frustration, while the blogger in extract 64 probably wants to show the continuity of the talking rather than suggesting any kind of frustration.

(63) We were then dragged out outside to wait wait wait.

{Yuhui Han, 23/5/06}

(64) Think it was a successful party. Met with old sec' school friends and talk talk talk.   {Shuyi, 12/6/06}

There is some debate about the origin of these kinds of reduplication. Wee (2004c) suggests that the intimacy of reduplicated nouns comes from Chinese while the continuity of repeated verbs originates from Malay, so there is evidence that Singapore English has been influenced by both languages. However, Ansaldo (2004) insists that Hokkien is the source of all kinds of reduplication, including the regular occurrence of tripled verbs.

Kachru (2005: 49) notes the use of reduplication in the English spoken in India, for adjectives in phrases such as *hot, hot coffee* and *small,*

small things, and also for verbs as in *to give crying crying* to capture the incessant nature of the crying. One wonders how extensive this feature is in the new varieties of English that are emerging around the world.

3.12 Tags

In Singapore, the final tags *is it* and *isn't it* tend to be used invariantly, regardless of the verb or the subject in the main clause. Although this is very common even in educated speech, there are no clear instances in the data for Hui Min, perhaps because question tags such as these only occur in more interactive data and not in the kind of long monologue represented by most of the data for her, where the interviewer only occasionally asks a question. There are no clear instances in the NIECSSE data either, because the Singapore speakers are mostly answering questions rather than asking them. A couple of examples from blogs are shown in extracts 65 and 66.

> (65) he think I want to listen to his story is it?   {Divya, 25/6/06}

> (66) It doesn't really matter what they think so much of you if you have a clear conscience isn't it?   {Gabe, 24/6/06}

Baskaran (2004b: 1080) observes that these invariant *is it* and *isn't it* tags are also found in Malaysian English, with such examples as 'He can play the piano, is it?', and Kachru (2005: 49) reports the use of the invariant *isn't it* tag in the English spoken in India, with examples such as 'You are going tomorrow, isn't it?' We might also note that use of *isn't it* (more often pronounced as [ɪnɪʔ] and written as *innit*) is common nowadays in many varieties of British English.

One other invariant tag that occurs quite regularly in Singapore is *right*. We find it twice in the data for Hui Min, in extracts 67 and 68.

> (67) before I graduate I'll definitely er visit there a few times, right . . . yah, mmm   {iF13-f:54}

> (68) that's the primary school I'm posted to, right . . . er . . . I don't know . . .   {iF13-g:199}

However, we should note that *right* is also common in other varieties of English, and Carter and McCarthy (2006) give the following excerpt of British English from a university science lecture, where there are five instances of *right* in seventy-one words:

We can then have toxic events. Right. These again can be direct. They can be subtle. But they cause lots and lots of injuries. Right. Here's an example of one. There's a section of normal liver. Right. The thing to notice is that all cells, all the cells look roughly the same. Right. So we've got at the top we've got portal triad. At the bottom we've got ventral vein. Right. (Carter and McCarthy 2006: 209)

Date (2005) comments on the use of a falling tone on *right* in Singapore English, as he would expect a rising tone on this word used as a tag, and indeed it is true that *right* in both extracts 67 and 68 is on a low pitch (202 Hz and 168 Hz respectively) with no hint of a rising tone. But is this really any different from the way it would occur in British English? Carter and McCarthy provide audio clips for their data, and of the five instances of *right* in the extract from a science lecture shown above, only the first and third have a rising tone while the other three have a falling tone. So it seems that the usage in Singapore may not in fact be any different from that found in Britain.

3.13 Extra prepositions and missing prepositions

In Singapore English, prepositions are occasionally not present when they would be expected in other varieties of English, and sometimes we also find extra prepositions. For instances of a missing prepositions, *to* is absent after *subscribe* in extract 69, and *for* does not occur after *applied* in extract 70.

(69) I didn't really subscribe any magazine previously   {iF13-b:145}

(70) so it's not because of I I was out of a job, then I applied teaching
   {iF13-e:169}

In extract 70, we might also note the extra preposition *of* after *because*. For further instances of extra prepositions, in data from blogs we find *emphasise on* in extract 71 and *discuss about* in extract 72. In both these cases, the verb would be transitive in most other varieties of English, so there would be no preposition between the verb and its object.

(71) I guess the way they are chosen is too harsh and they don't emphasise on the correct stuff.   {Timmy Goh, 11/6/06}

(72) I will not discuss about the level of courtesy exhibited by the average Singaporean   {gaussito, 24/6/06}

Notice that use of these prepositions with the corresponding nouns would be expected in British or American English where *emphasis on* and *discussion about* are the normal collocations, so in extending the use of a preposition to the verbs, Singapore English might be seen as regularising the language. We might also note that if we substitute *focus* for *emphasise* in extract 71, then 'they don't focus on the correct stuff' is perfectly standard, and similarly substituting *talk* for *discuss* in extract 72 results in 'I will not talk about the level of courtesy' which is also standard, so there is nothing inherently illogical about using similar prepositions with *emphasise* and *discuss*. It is just that English is highly idiosyncratic, and it seems that Singapore English occasionally irons out a few of the creases in the fabric of the language. As this is one of the normal ways in which languages change (Aitchison 2001: 204), maybe preposition usage is one of the areas where Singapore is at the forefront of the natural development of English.

3.14 Null subjects

In standard English, every finite verb must have a subject. Although null-subject structures like 'Went to the market' might be common in diary entries and also as truncated responses in conversations, they would be rare in British or American English for the kind of extended monologue exemplified by the data from Hui Min.

In contrast, in Singapore English null-subject sentences are very common. Gupta (1994: 10) lists their occurrence as one of the diagnostic features for colloquial Singapore English, but the educated Singapore English data from Hui Min also exhibits very frequent instances of null-subject structures, and this even extends to her rather more formal conversation with her expatriate tutor in the NIECSSE data (Tan 2003). Extracts 73 to 76 illustrate the use of null-subject structures in the speech of Hui Min, and extract 77 is from her interview in the NIECSSE data. (We will compare the use of null subjects in these two sources of data in more detail when we discuss variation in Singapore English in Chapter 5.) In all cases, the first-person subject is omitted because it is obvious from the context that the speaker is talking about herself, and it seems that inclusion of the subject is unnecessary if it can be determined from context. (Instances of an omitted subject are indicated by the symbol 'Ø'.)

(73) so in the end . . . Ø didn't didn't try out the rides so initially Ø want to take the ferris wheel . . . but then . . . the queue is very long and too expensive ((laughs)) so Ø didn't, didn't take any . . . Ø spent about two hours there looking at the things   {iF13-a:70}

(74) so Ø only tried one or two dishes, Ø didn't really do much cooking

{iF13-b:47}

(75) then other than that . . . mmm . . . Ø play with my niece and nephews
. . . yup . . . Ø bring them out . . . to the library   {iF13-b:107}

(76) because during . . . school time Ø hardly had time to watch any movies

{iF13-b:213}

(77) Yeah, Ø can cycle, not very well, but Ø can cycle, ah, Ø knocked myself
against a pillar . . . but ((laughs)) then Ø managed to pick up ((laughs))
cycling.   {NIECSSE, F13-c:02}

In fact, in the one hour of data for Hui Min, there are sixty-nine
instances of null-subject structures (Tan 2007). Two questions can be
asked about this phenomenon: first, where does it come from; and
second, what is it about the structure of Singapore English that allows
for null-subject sentences.

Bao (2001) assumes that, since the majority of the population of
Singapore is ethnically Chinese and most nowadays speak Mandarin, the
source of null-subject structures in Singapore English must be a variety
of Chinese, and he examines the existence of null-subject sentences in
Mandarin in some depth. While it is certainly true that subjects are often
absent in Mandarin when they can be determined from context (Li and
Thompson, 1981: 657), we should remember that until the 1980s very
few people in Singapore spoke Mandarin, so it is important to examine
Hokkien, which was originally the most commonly spoken variety of
Chinese. Indeed, Hokkien is characterised by many null-subject structures, such as the following from Taiwanese Hokkien (Taiwan Language
Committee 2005: 67). Notice that the English gloss in each case has a
subject pronoun but the Hokkien does not have one.

dai bak	cia tau	bhe	an zua^n	ki
Taipei	station	will	how	go

'How do I get to Taipei Train Station?'

ze	gong cia	ah si	ze	ziat un	long ma	e sai
take	bus	or	take	metro	both	can

'You can take either the bus or metro.'

However, although it is certainly true that all varieties of Chinese are
characterised by null-subject structures, so is Malay, and as in the past

Singapore English was closely linked to Malaysian English and the two varieties have only recently diverged, it is likely that Malay has also influenced the occurrence of null subjects in Singapore English. The following is an example of null-subject usage in Malay (Deterding and Poedjosoedarmo 2001: 177). Note that the English gloss has three tokens of the first-person pronoun, but the Malay has none.

Ingat-ingat,	waktu	masih	kecil,	sering	pergi	memancing.
remember	when	still	small	often	go	fishing

'I remember, when I was still small, I often went fishing.'

It is in fact likely that both Malay and Chinese have influenced the sentence structure of Singapore English (Poedjosoedarmo 2000a), and furthermore it seems true that a feature is most likely to be adopted into a local variety of English when it occurs in more than one indigenous language. In Chapter 4, we will find other possible examples of the combined influence of Chinese and Malay on Singapore English when we consider topic prominence and also the discourse particle *lah*.

The second question that arises regarding null-subject sentences is why they exist in Singapore English, and this issue has some theoretical significance for the structure of language. It is sometimes assumed that a language with a rich system of present-tense inflections, such as Italian, Spanish or Portuguese, is also likely to be characterised by null-subject structures because the subject can be identified unambiguously from the verb endings. In contrast, English has an impoverished system of verbal inflections, which means that if the subject is omitted, its referent cannot generally be established from the endings on the verb. Radford (1997) has shown that, in Shakespeare's time, there was a relatively rich system of inflections in English and null-subject sentences were also acceptable, but with the loss of the second-person singular pronoun *thou*, the inflections became impoverished, and so a subject gradually became obligatory for English. We have seen that the use of present-tense verbal inflections in educated Singapore English is basically rather similar to standard English, so how is it that Singapore English allows such frequent null-subject structures?

To answer this question, we need to consider the structure of Chinese, which has no verbal inflections but nevertheless is characterised by regular null-subject structures. One possible explanation for this is that Chinese is typologically a topic-comment language in contrast with the basic subject-verb-object structure of English sentences (Li and Thompson 1981: 15), and in Chinese once the topic is established, there is no need for it to be repeated. According to this analysis, null-subject structures may occur in rich inflection languages such as Italian or topic-prominent languages like Chinese, but not in English which has neither rich inflections nor topic prominence (Tan 2007). The interesting thing here is that Singapore English also has frequent instances of topic fronting, so just like Chinese it might be regarded as a topic-prominent language. As topic prominence is concerned with discourse, we will consider it in some detail in Chapter 4.

4 Discourse and Lexis

The boundary between syntax and discourse is somewhat fuzzy. Discourse deals with the order of presentation of ideas, but syntax is concerned with word order and clearly this has a big influence on the way that concepts are presented. In general, discourse takes a larger picture, analysing the way that the text develops, but inevitably there is a degree of overlap.

In the previous chapter under the heading of syntax, null-subject structures were discussed. However, one of the puzzles is why null-subject sentences are acceptable in Singapore English but not in British or American English even though all these varieties have a similar system of present-tense verbal inflections, and topic prominence was suggested as having an influence on this. The fronting of a topic belongs within the realm of discourse, because it involves manipulating word order to present ideas in a certain way, so it will be covered in this chapter.

After topic prominence has been discussed, we will consider the use of resumptive pronouns, tolerance for repetition of words, and the ubiquitous occurrence of discourse particles such as *lah*, *ah*, and also *yah*. Then we will proceed to deal with individual words, both those that are unique to Singapore English as a result of borrowing, compounding, or use of abbreviations, and also those that are found in other varieties of English but are used in a different way in Singapore.

4.1 Topic prominence

There is a tendency in Singapore English for the topic to occur very prominently at the front of an utterance. This is probably influenced by the basic topic-comment nature of Chinese, but Singapore English may additionally be influenced by the fact that Malay is also a topic-prominent language. Alsagoff (1992: 84) gives the following example of a fronted topic in Malay:

Doktor itu	saya	cubit.
doctor the	I	pinch

'I pinched the doctor.'

For the data of Hui Min, an example of a topic placed clearly at the front of an utterance is *magazines* in extract 1.

(1) magazines, OK, er I I ... I didn't really subscribe any magazine previously   {iF13-b:134}

In extract 1, the topicalised word *magazines* is repeated in the main part of the utterance, but sometimes the topic is one of the constituents of the sentence and is not repeated, as in extract 2 where the fronted constituent *the whole process* is the object of *break down*.

(2) so the whole process I need to break down for the different operators
{iF13-e:77}

This process of fronting an object can also occur in British usage, particularly in spoken language (Carter and McCarthy 2006: 192), but perhaps it is a little more common in Singapore English. (It would be interesting to test this, but we would need some figures on the occurrence of fronting in British English before we determine if the frequency in Singapore English really is higher.)

In addition, at the front of an utterance in Singapore English, we often find a phrase that provides a topic for the rest without necessarily being a constituent of the main clause, so in these circumstances it cannot really be analysed as something that is fronted. Sometimes, at least for the speech of Hui Min, this constituent is indicated by the topic-marking *-wise* suffix, as with *colleagues-wise* and *shopping-wise* in extracts 3 and 4, but in other cases it is not marked in any particular way, for example, with *Australia* and *this new campus* in extracts 5 and 6. Later in this chapter, we will see how the particle *ah* can also serve to mark the topic at the front of an utterance.

(3) colleagues-wise, I enjoy teaching in erm Princess E   {iF13-a:220}

(4) shopping-wise, nothing much to buy there lah, basically
{iF13-c:123}

(5) Australia, I've been to Sydney . . . and Perth   {iF13-d:05}

(6) er this new campus, I guess, mmm . . . I guess I like the library the most, yah   {iF13-f:05}

In the previous chapter, we discussed the issue of why null-subject structures are acceptable in Singapore English, and we can now consider more fully the contribution that topic prominence might play. It has previously been suggested that it is topic prominence that allows null subjects to occur in Chinese, and Tan (2007) investigated the data from Hui Min, to see if the same link can be established for Singapore English. He hypothesised that, if the two phenomena are linked, then stretches of discourse that have frequent topic fronting might also be characterised by null subjects. He further suggested that if the two features are characteristic of informal Singapore English rather than standard English, then they might both occur more frequently in light-hearted conversations and be relatively absent from discussions involving more serious issues. However, for the data of Hui Min, he actually found little correlation between the occurrence of topic prominence and null-subject structures or between the frequency of these two features and the seriousness of the conversation. One possible explanation is that there is, in fact, little shift in the style of speech throughout the data, as during the whole one hour of conversation, Hui Min is chatting to her good friend in the same location, so even though she talks about a wide range of different things, there is not enough variation in the conversational setting to result in any substantial shift in style. What is certainly true is that prominent topics at the front of utterances and null subjects both occur quite regularly in the speech of Hui Min, and so a link between the two phenomena remains a real possibility. One might conclude that it may not be a coincidence that both topic prominence and null subjects are very frequent in this style of speech, but further research is needed involving a wide range of different speakers to establish if a link between the two phenomena does exist.

4.2 Resumptive pronouns

In some utterances, following a fronted topic we find a pronoun that refers back to the topic, a 'resumptive pronoun', and even though this is also related to topic prominence, we might note that it results in an additional pronoun rather than the absent pronoun that was discussed in the previous chapter under the heading of null-subject structures. Illustrations of resumptive pronouns are found in extracts 7 and 8 where *they* refers back to the fronted topic *my sisters*, in extract 9 where *she* refers back to *my sister*, and in extract 10 where *he* refers to *my brother*.

> (7) basically my sisters, they will buy magazines like Her World, Cleo, er
>   female magazines, yah   {iF13-b:140}

(8) then er, two of my sisters, they're already married   {iF13-k:37}

(9) so er my my sister, one of my sister . . . she actually stayed next door
to to us   {iF13-k:55}

(10) my brother, he he has signed on with SAF   {iF13-k:187}

Baskaran (2004b) observes that usage such as this is common in Malaysian English but that it might be a normal pragmatic strategy for contrastive purposes, which suggests that it may not in fact represent anything unusual for the English found in the region. Indeed, Carter and McCarthy (2006: 193) report that use of a pronoun to refer back to fronted elements like these (which they call 'headers') is common in spoken British English. Further work is needed to determine if the frequency of occurrence of resumptive pronouns is greater in Singapore and Malaysian English than in other varieties of the language.

4.3 Tolerance for repetition

In Chapter 2, mention was made of the lack of deaccenting, as lexical items may receive substantial prominence even when they are repeated. In fact, there is a general tolerance for repetition of words in Singapore English in instances where other varieties of English might use pronouns or ellipsis. For example, note how many times the word *magazine(s)* occurs in both extracts 11 and 12.

(11) magazines, OK, er I I . . . I didn't really subscribe any magazine previously . . . basically my sisters, they will buy . . . magazines like Her World, Cleo, er female magazines, yah   {iF13-b:134}

(12) and then er magazines, yah magazines like Her World, or other magazines ah, any magazines   {iF13-b:52}

Similarly we find repetition of *campus* in extract 13, and *maths* in extract 14.

(13) but comparing this campus with the old campus, I think I like the old campus in the sense, it has its unique . . . look lor   {iF13-f:138}

(14) then for maths, I guess I did A-level maths so . . . erm . . . it'll be easier for me to do maths, yah, i- at NIE, as compared to taking up geography or history or literature which I had little erm . . . knowledge of . . . yah, so I chose maths and . . . maths basically is about doing tutorials   {iF13-g:33}

This seems to reflect a pattern in Mandarin Chinese, where even in formal written texts, lexical repetition is tolerated while use of pronouns, especially the inanimate third-person pronoun *ta* (它), is less common. In fact, in Chinese, cohesion is often achieved by means of repetition of words, and this can cause a problem in translation from Chinese to English, as alternatives for direct lexical repetition have to be found.

4.4 The discourse particle *lah*

Perhaps the one word that is most emblematic of Singapore English is the discourse particle *lah*. Lim (2001) describes it as the very icon of the English of Singapore and Malaysia, though of course this reflects the fact that it occurs very regularly not just in Singapore but also in Malaysian English.

There can be a wide range of different functions for *lah*, including to soften the force of an utterance and also to create a feeling of solidarity (Richards and Tay 1977), though a stressed version of *lah* may sometimes have exactly the opposite meaning, creating a social distance and signalling power (Bell and Ser 1983).

Although use of discourse particles is one of the diagnostics of colloquial Singapore English suggested by Gupta (1994: 10), *lah* and *ah* are so pervasive that they also sometimes occur in educated Singapore English. Deterding and Low (2003) report twenty-eight tokens of these two particles in the four hours of conversation in the NIECSSE data, even though these recordings mostly involve university undergraduates talking to their expatriate tutor when presumably the speakers were using a formal register of their language.

In the one hour of data for Hui Min, there are forty-seven instances of *lah*, including those in extracts 15 to 17. In all these instances, as the tone of the conversation is always quite relaxed, one assumes that the function of *lah* is to build solidarity between the speaker and her friend, and none of the instances discussed here is intended to signal power or increase social distance.

(15) a lot of things to do *lah*, so didn't really enjoy the three weeks there
{iF13-a:135}

(16) I have been to quite a few countries, er er erm . . . previously *lah* . . . these two years I've not . . . been travelling much because er, no income
{iF13-c:05}

(17) till now the baby is still not so bad *lah*, because basically . . . he will cry when he he he need food . . . or attention
{iF13-c:103}

There has been considerable discussion in the literature about the different variants of *lah*. Kwan-Terry (1978) identifies two types of *lah*, the stressed and the unstressed versions, and Bell and Ser (1983) suggest that these two may be distinguished by means of length, with the stressed version being about twice as long as the unstressed one. Furthermore, Loke and Low (1988) propose that there are at least nine separate tonal variants of *lah*, all indicating different pragmatic functions.

The high-quality recording conditions of the data for Hui Min offer an opportunity to investigate the variants of *lah* in some detail, particularly regarding pitch movements during the course of the word. For all forty-seven tokens of *lah* in the data of Hui Min, the fundamental frequency in Hz (the acoustic correlate of pitch) was measured at the start and end of the particle and also compared with the fundamental frequency at the end of the preceding word. Results show that there is an average fall of 17 Hz from the previous word to the start of the particle, and there are no clear instances of an increase in pitch between the two words. So it seems that *lah* generally begins on a lower pitch than the previous word, though it does sometimes start on the same level. For the pitch movement during the particle itself, there is an average fall in fundamental frequency of 20 Hz, though some tokens have a clear fall while others have a level pitch. We will now investigate this tonal movement during the particle in more detail.

The only token that has a clear rising pitch (of 42 Hz) is that in extract 18, but perceptually this rise seems to be in preparation for the continuing discourse rather than indicating any special meaning for the particle.

> (18) but I guess the tough thing would be . . . learning it learning it . . . at
> the beginning *lah*, and erm . . . buying the the the equipment . . . would
> be quite expensive also, yah   {iF13-i:24}

Before we look at the patterns for the tokens of *lah* in general, we may note that *OK lah* is quite a frequent collocation, as shown in extracts 19 to 23. In these five extracts, the phrase always occurs after a pause, and the *lah* seems to add a certain degree of reservation, maybe indicating that the speaker is not too sure that the matter being described really is OK. Note that in three of the extracts, we also find *I guess*, further hedging the degree of certainty being expressed. Hui Min was in fact subsequently asked about the meaning of *OK lah*, and she suggested that it is 'something like an obligatory okay', which perhaps is similar to an OK with reservation.

(19) Japan is . . . mmm . . . OK *lah* the countryside is . . . is nice, yup

{iF13-c:224}

(20) Taiwan . . . OK *lah* . . . er how to say . . . er . . . nothing nothing impressed me over there   {iF13-c:281}

(21) the people . . . OK *lah* I guess I didn't really erm . . . er because . . . it was really a big group   {iF13-d:36}

(22) I do enjoy talking to them at times *lah*, yah, er yup but . . . OK *lah* I guess   {iF13-e:288}

(23) I guess arts . . . OK *lah*, one thing I can enjoy, I mean maybe I will like arts is that it's not exam   {iF13-h:264}

So let us first consider the pitch movements on this phrase. In all five tokens of *OK lah*, the particle starts on quite a high pitch (average 262 Hz) and then there is a substantial fall during the *lah* (average 46 Hz). However, to understand the tonal contour on *lah*, we need to consider the pitch movement on *OK* as well. A typical pattern is illustrated in Figure 4.1 (from extract 21), where it can be seen that there is a mid-level pitch on *O*, a high pitch on *K*, and a fall on *lah*. We might call this a mid-high-fall contour over the phrase. In fact the same mid-high-fall contour is found on all five instances of *OK lah*.

This seems to suggest that the falling pitch movement on *lah* arises because of the mid-high pitch contour on *OK*, so perhaps this word has

Figure 4.1 Waveform (top panel) and pitch track (bottom panel) for the token of *OK lah* from iF13-d:36. The plot was generated using Praat (Boersma and Weenink 2005).

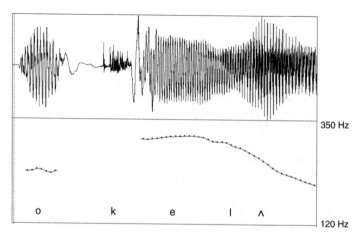

a fixed tone, reminiscent of the lexical tones of Chinese. However, in the data for Hui Min, there are eighteen tokens of *OK* apart from those with a following *lah*, and in only six of these eighteen tokens is there a clear mid-high intonation, so it appears that this contour is not found on most instances of *OK*. One alternative possibility is that the mid-high-fall contour on the phrase *OK lah* is an idiosyncratic pattern that occurs especially on this phrase, the sort of stylised contour that is found in English when calling someone's name or in conventional greetings such as *good morning* (Cruttenden 1997: 120). This stylised contour on *OK lah* seems natural for Singapore English and not some kind of idiosyncratic usage by Hui Min, but further research is needed to confirm if it is indeed shared by other speakers and furthermore if the contour extends to any other common phrases.

Now let us consider the pitch movement on some other tokens of *lah*. We will attempt to investigate the issue by identifying a few distinct tonal contours, selecting four clear instances of each contour, and then seeing if we can detect any difference in meaning between them. The three tonal contours we will investigate are: falling tone, low-level tone, and mid-level tone. The four selected falls (which exclude the instances of *OK lah* as they have already been discussed) are shown in extracts 24 to 27. All of them have a fall in fundamental frequency of at least 40 Hz over the duration of the *lah*, and the average starting point is quite high at 240 Hz, so they all involve a fall from a high starting point.

(24) then I will just erm . . . take the opportunity to to read them *lah*. . .yeah
      . . . erm   {iF13-b:146}

(25) usually you will be . . . squashed . . . ((laughs)) during the early hours
      lah when they're on their wa-   {iF13-c:252}

(26) yeah, so as to get a place . . . for myself *lah* in primary school, rather
      than secondary school   {iF13-g:163}

(27) my feet stopped kicking, so basically I I . . . so basically I sink *lah*. . . so
      ((laughs)) I struggle   {iF13-i:158}

Extracts 28 to 31 are the clearest instances of a low-level tone on *lah*. They have an insignificant average rise of 4 Hz in fundamental frequency, and the average starting point is 178 Hz, much lower than the 240 Hz starting point for the falls.

(28) shopping-wise, nothing much to buy there *lah*. . . basically . . . yup . . .
      then . . . mmm the other trip I liked . . . was to Nepal   {iF13-c:123}

(29) we will move around in one big group *lah* . . . yah, so . . . didn't really interact much with the local people there {iF13-d:52}

(30) lecture halls . . . alright *lah*, compared to the old . . . old lecture halls we have {iF13-f:84}

(31) you feel comfortable there . . . yah . . . mmm, maybe I'm old also *lah* . . . ((laughs)) that's why {iF13-f:152}

Finally, extracts 32 to 35 are the clearest instances of a mid-level tone on *lah*. They have an insignificant average fall of 3 Hz in fundamental frequency during the particle, and the average starting point is 209 Hz, which is substantially higher than the 178 Hz for the low-level examples.

(32) next time when you get married, you'll know how to cook ((laugh)) . . . so, um yeah *lah*, so only tried one or two dishes {iF13-b:42}

(33) they do have shopping area *lah*, yah . . . but not really like big shopping centre {iF13-d:130}

(34) yah, I guess s-, basically it's because it's scenic *lah* . . . yah, I think one place that I can compare with Switzerland easily {iF13-d:272}

(35) was thinking, OK, just try *lah* . . . yah, then quite a few of my friends are in here also {iF13-h:48}

Is there any difference in meaning between those three kinds of *lah*? The falls seem to involve more assertiveness, particularly extracts 24 and 27; the low-levels may indicate a resigned acceptance, especially 28 and 31; and the mid-levels seem to carry more of a note of cheerful resignation, especially 32 and 35. However, does this mean that there really are three variants of *lah*, or is this particle just a vehicle to carry the intonation that is evident at that point in the discourse? It is hard to be certain, especially on the basis of the limited range of data analysed here. We really need some instances of *lah* being used in pleading, cajoling, teasing, complaining and other such environments.

Another measurement one might attempt is duration. Although there is indeed substantial variation in the duration of *lah*, ranging from 275 msec down to 100 msec or less, this seems to depend mostly on whether the word occurs before a pause or not. It is therefore hard to ascribe any special meaning for it, especially given the frequency of final lengthening in Singapore English that was discussed in Chapter 2. So it is not possible to evaluate whether there really are a long and a short variant of *lah*, as suggested by Bell and Ser (1983).

We will now consider the origin of this *lah* particle that is so common in the English of Singapore and also Malaysia. Bodman (1955: 45–6) lists various final particles in Hokkien, including *la* which generally follows verbs and has a perfective meaning (equivalent to Mandarin *le* 了), so this is certainly one candidate for the origin of *lah* in Singapore and Malaysian English, even though the Hokkien particle discussed by Bodman has a rather more restricted occurrence. In fact, Richards and Tay (1977) claim that the Hokkien particle has a much wider range of uses than a simple perfective verbal affix, so they suggest that it is indeed the origin of Singaporean *lah*. Another possible source is Cantonese, where the *la* particle helps to carry a mood of cordial invitation or cheerful acceptance (Tong and James 1994: 17, 125). In fact, Brown (1999: 127) suggests that the Singapore *lah* particle may come from a number of different Chinese languages but he states that it is not related to the *lah* particle found in Malay.

However, some others believe that the *lah* particle that is common in colloquial Malay may indeed be the source. Liaw (1999: 259) states that one of the functions of the *lah* particle in Malay is to 'soften the tone of requests, commands, invitations, prohibitions, etc' which seems close to some of its observed functions in Singapore English, and Morais (2001) lists Malaysian English *lah* as originating from Malay.

In fact, there is also some disagreement about the origins of *lah* in Malay. Richards and Tay (1977) propose that it originates from Hokkien, but Teoh et al. (2003) suggest exactly the opposite, claiming that the *lah* that is found in the Hokkien of Penang is a loanword from Malay and stating that its prolific use in Penang is strong evidence for the influence of Malay on the variety of Hokkien spoken there.

In conclusion, we really do not know where *lah* comes from. One possibility is that *lah* in Singapore and Malaysian English comes from a variety of sources, and Baskaran (2004b) suggests that although it may come from Hokkien, the influence of Malay cannot be discounted. In this respect, *lah* might be similar to so many other features of Singapore English – such as the null-subject structures discussed in the previous chapter, and the frequent fronted topics considered earlier in this chapter – as it is probable that a word or grammatical feature that is matched in more than one indigenous language (such as Hokkien, Cantonese and Malay) is most likely to be absorbed into Singapore English. Multiple sources for a feature might be quite common, and it may be misguided to try to identify a single source.

4.5 Other discourse particles

Another common particle in Singapore English is *ah*. In the data for Hui Min, there are twenty-three instances of *ah*, and many of these have a grammatical role, to mark off the topic of an utterance (Deterding and Low 2003) and to indicate that something more is to follow (Low and Brown 2005: 176). Some instances of *ah* in the speech of Hui Min are found in extracts 36 to 39.

(36) which subject *ah* . . . I guess I have no preference now, I hope I will enjoy teaching all . . . all of them {iF13-h:251}

(37) reading, *ah*, I guess, erm . . . fictions {iF13-f:236}

(38) magazines, *ah*, magazines . . . er . . . mmm . . . all sorts lah, I guess I would try to read . . . all kinds of . . . magazines {iF13-f:270}

(39) my fravourite subject to teach *ah* . . . aiya ((tsk)) . . . don't know lah, I guess . . . mmm . . . I thought maths would be something easy to teach {iF13-h:199}

The discourse particle *ah* also sometimes occurs in the speech of Hui Min in the NIECSSE data, as is illustrated in extracts 40 and 41 (though the particle in extract 41 might be *lah* instead). We will return to a comparison of the occurrence of discourse particles in the relatively informal recording and the more formal NIECSSE data when we consider shifts in style in Chapter 5.

(40) yah, can cycle, not very well, but can cycle *ah*, knocked myself against a pillar {NIECSSE, F13-c:05}

(41) Japan, actually . . . did a lot of shopping *(l)ah*, window shopping actually {NIECSSE, F13-g:01}

One other particle that occurs sometimes in the data for Hui Min is *lor*, as in extract 42. (To be honest, some of the instances of *lah* listed above might also be shown as *lor* instead. It is not clear how distinct these two particles really are.) Low and Brown (2005: 178) suggest that *lor* expresses resignation. Perhaps here it is intended to convey a degree of frustration, as the speaker cannot think how to express herself clearly.

(42) I think I like the old campus in the sense, it has its unique . . . look *lor*, I don't know how to say {iF13-f:141}

In fact, in Singapore English there are more particles than the three illustrated here. Gupta (1992b) discusses eleven different particles, including *what*, *ma* and *mei*, but perhaps these occur in more interactive situations than the extended monologue of the data from Hui Min.

4.6 *Yah*

The particle *yah* (or its variant *yup*) occurs very regularly in Singapore English, but in contrast to particles such as *lah* and *ah*, it is not just a feature of Singapore and Malaysian English because it also occurs frequently in other varieties of English, such as the speech of young people in Britain, as we will see below.

Apart from its obvious function of answering a question (being equivalent to *yes*), there appear to be two main roles for *yah*: to signal continuation, and to indicate completion. These two contrasting uses are illustrated in extract 43, where the first *yah* is followed immediately by 'because the blade looks sharp', but the second *yah* comes at the end of this stretch of speech. The difference between these two functions of *yah* may lie in the intonation they carry: the first one is on a level pitch, while the second one carries a falling tone.

(43) skating, ice-skating, it looks to me a very dangerous sport . . . *yah* because the blade looks so sharp, I mean it's like if you fall another person will will will will ((laugh)) may just, erm, how to say ((laugh)), may just erm cut you with their their blades when they erm . . . er move past you . . . *yah*.   {iF13-i:277}

Sometimes *yah* occurs rather often in a stretch of discourse, such as the six tokens (and also one of *yup*) in 109 words in extract 44.

(44) my mum usually erm . . . most of, nowadays she . . . she look after my niece and nephews *yah*, last time . . . erm . . . she will um babysit for other people, *yah* when erm . . . all of us, as in myself and my sisters and brothers er were studying, *yah* still studying, so . . . she will have additional income by babysitting other people's erm . . . children, *yup*, so erm . . . *yah*, that was like a long way back, when I was in primary school, *yah* . . . so, erm nowadays some of the kids that she have brought up, actually do keep in tou- contact with her, *yah*, and at times they will come and visit her, during Chinese New Year   {iF13-l:02}

Altogether, there are 260 tokens of *yah* and sixty-five of *yup* in the one hour of speech from Hui Min, which means that these particles are substantially more common than the forty-seven instances of *lah* and twenty-three instances of *ah*.

However, we must be cautious about attributing a special status to *yah* in Singapore English. Although for British English Carter and McCarthy (2006: 198) give the normal function of *yeah* (which is presumably quite similar) as checking that something has been understood, they also give an example of *oh yeah* to mark the link between an interrupted topic and its resumption, and this seems quite similar to the linking function of *yah* observed here (2006: 218). Indeed, Stenström et al. (2002) observe that *yeah* is very common as a linking device in the speech of young British speakers, and they offer the following example:

> This geezer from Bedlam yeah got stopped the other day in this car yeah, he was pissed, he was tripping and he was speeding yeah, no MOT, no licence, no tax, no road insurance yeah. (Stenström et al. 2002: 172)

Notice that, just as with Singapore English, in this example of British English *yeah* occurs both in the middle of a stretch of discourse and also at the end, as a continuation particle and a completion particle.

It is interesting to note that, in Singapore English, the particles *lah* (which often comes at the end) and *ah* (which generally indicates something is to follow) are usually regarded as constituting part of the colloquial variety of the language (even if they also sometimes appear in more formal usage), while the *yah* particle is regarded as more standard even though it seems to carry similar kinds of meaning as *lah* and *ah*. Certainly, there is a difference between them, as *lah* in particular serves to soften the tone of an utterance and build solidarity between speakers, while *yah* is mainly a linking or completion particle, but inherently there does not seem to be much difference in their functions as discourse particles.

4.7 Borrowed words

The particle *lah* is almost certainly borrowed from local languages even if we cannot be sure which ones. We will now consider some other borrowed words.

In the analysis of language, it is sometimes difficult to separate borrowed words from language mixing. However, for ethnically Chinese speakers of Singapore English, the distinction is quite straightforward, as words that are borrowed are always either from Malay or from a regional variety of Chinese, usually Hokkien or Cantonese, but in the younger generation, language mixing generally involves Mandarin. It seems that there is as yet almost no borrowing from Mandarin into Singapore

English, but even Malay or Indian Singaporeans will all be familiar with some Hokkien terms such as *kiasu* ('afraid to lose out') or *angmoh* ('foreigner', literally 'red hair').

In the data from Hui Min, there are just two instances of Mandarin words and no borrowings from Hokkien (apart from discourse particles). In extract 45, we find *luo-han-yu* (a kind of fish especially prized by collectors), and in extract 46, there is *pen-zai* ('bonzai', where the Chinese word is of course itself borrowed from Japanese). When inserting these two words into English, the speaker maintains the original Mandarin tones, and both of them occur because she cannot think of the English equivalent. In fact, for *luo-han-yu* there is no common equivalent in English, although in extract 46, Hui Min does remember the English word *bonzai* immediately afterwards. One can conclude that these are instances of language mixing, not borrowing, especially as both words are spoken clearly and precisely with the Mandarin tones intact.

(45) he's keeping a few fish ... nowadays, yah you heard of *luo-han-yu*, I don't know what you call that in English   {iF13-k:241}

(46) he do some ... er ... *pen-zai* ah, bonzai ah, you call that {iF13-k:260}

Even though borrowings from Malay, Hokkien and Cantonese seem to be absent from the data of Hui Min, they are very common in Singapore English. In extract 47 from the NIECSSE data, M13, who is ethnically Chinese, uses the Malay word *kampung* ('village').

(47) I was born in a *kampung*... somewhere in Novena ...
                                        {NIECSSE, M13-h:25}

Perhaps the most common kind of borrowing involves food and food-related items. In fact, the Malay word *makan* ('eat') is used very regularly in Singapore English, as in the data from blogs in extracts 48 and 49.

(48) After returning the stuff to them, we went to makan at Jurong entertainment centre.   {Ning, 15/6/06}

(49) he fetched me at clementi and we makan at the coffeeshop around there   {shygal001, 22/6/06}

Extract 50 includes another instance of borrowing involving food. Although the speaker is ethnically Chinese, she uses the Malay words *pasar malam* ('night market') when she talks about what she likes to eat in Kuala Lumpur.

(50) it's cheaper and um . . . the food over . . . at the . . . those wet markets
you know those *pasar malam* markets . . . are very much better I think
{NIECSSE, F1-b:28}

4.8 Compounds

Some compound phrases have been created in Singapore to describe aspects of the local environment or culture. For example, in extract 50 above, a *wet market* is a local-style market selling vegetables, fish and meat, and if we look at the continuation of this utterance, in extract 51, the speaker also uses *hawker centre* to refer to a cheap food centre with lots of different stalls offering a variety of food.

(51) the food over . . . at the . . . those wet markets you know those *pasar malam* markets . . . are very much better I think . . . but not the food over in the hawker centre . . . the restaurants   {NIECSSE, F1-b:30}

Although it is true that the speaker is discussing food in Malaysia at this point, the terms *wet market* and *hawker centre* are also very commonly used in Singapore. In fact, the speaker hesitates when saying *hawker centre*, possibly because she is not sure whether the term is appropriate for the places she goes to in Kuala Lumpur, and then she selects *restaurants* instead.

Another Singaporean compound is *void deck*, describing the empty space kept for social functions on the ground floor of most apartment blocks. This is illustrated in the data from a blog in extract 52.

(52) They must have broken into my neighbour's flat! I could not hesitate any longer. I called for the police using a public phone at the void deck of my block.   {WseeH, 2/6/06}

4.9 Clippings

Shortening of words by means of clipping is a well established means of creating new words, so in most varieties of English we have *fridge* from *refrigerator* and *flu* from *influenza*. Singapore has its own clippings, such as *aircon* from *air-conditioner*, as in extract 53, though we should note that *aircon* is also found in Hong Kong (Bolton 2003: 212) and the Philippines (Bautista 1997: 60) as well as in American English.

(53) the tutorial rooms are new, and er . . . the aircons are . . . it's always working . . . compared to the old campus, yup   {iF13-f:70}

Similarly, in the NIECSSE data we find *certificate* clipped to *cert* in extract 54 (by an ethnically Malay speaker), and the use of *zomb* from *zombie* in extract 55.

(54) just snorkeling, because we haven't got our er . . . dive cert yet
{NIECSSE, F16-b:40}

(55) once I get home I need a rest . . . I just zomb out I don't . . . I don't read I don't do anything, I just either watch TV or just stare at the wall
{NIECSSE, F19-f:26}

In fact, *zomb* should perhaps be regarded as an instance of a back-formation rather than a clipping (just as *opt* is a back-formation from *option* in standard English), as the word class has changed: *zombie* is a noun while *zomb* seems to be used as a verb in extract 55.

4.10 Initialisms

Acronyms are words created out of initials, so *scuba* [skubə] is derived from *self-contained underwater breathing apparatus*, and more recently *SARS* [sʌz] comes from *severe acute respiratory syndrome*. A similar process involving abbreviations based on initial letters is extremely common in Singapore, but these abbreviations are usually spelled out using the letter names, so the *PIE* (for the *Pan-Island Expressway*) is pronounced [pi ai i] rather than *[pai], and the ruling political party *PAP* (*People's Action Party*) is [pi e pi] and never *[pɛp]. Some people refer to these as acronyms, but as they are pronounced by means of the names of the initial letters, we will here call them 'initialisms'.

The data of Hui Min reveals a few uses of initialisms in extracts 56 to 58, including *AS* to refer to an *academic subject*, *NIE* for the *National Institute of Education*, *ACJC* for *Anglo-Chinese Junior College*, *JC* for *junior college*, and *SAF* to refer to the *Singapore Armed Forces*.

(56) so that's why I chose English as . . . the first AS, yah, to do in NIE
{iF13-g:26}

(57) I had swimming lessons at erm . . . ACJC during my JC time
{iF13-i:73}

(58) my brother, he he has signed on with SAF   {iF13-k:187}

We also find many uses of initialisms in the NIECSSE data. In extract 59, F6 (who is ethnically Malay) uses *MOE* to refer to the *Ministry of*

Education, and in extracts 60 to 63, other speakers use *HDB* (pronounced [hetʃ di bi]) to refer to the *Housing Development Board* (which provides government-built housing), *CPF* for the *Central Providence Fund* (the compulsory savings fund for all Singaporeans), *MRT* for the *Mass Rapid Transport* subway system, and *ROM* to refer to the *Registry of Marriages* (and, by extension, to the act of officially getting married). In fact all of these initialisms occur in official government usage as well in as the conversations of ordinary Singaporeans.

(59) maybe even if I were to quit teaching like say resign from MOE . . . probably I will still . . . do you know erm get involved in certain kind of . . . teaching   {NIECSSE, F6-h:10}

(60) the new HDB flats are usually smaller . . . so er that's why we . . . get an executive flat you see   {NIECSSE, F25-c:07}

(61) we have to use up all the CPF, but it's still not sufficient, so . . . er we have to . . . loan from the government   {NIECSSE, F25-d:14}

(62) I live in Toa Payoh erm . . . in a way it's quite conveniently situated in the sense that it's near the MRT . . . and the bus interchanges
                           {NIECSSE, F19-e:01}

(63) I am actually planning to get married . . . so I'll be having my ROM in December   {NIECSSE, F30-c:05}

Often initial letters are also used to refer to the names of cities in Malaysia, such as *KL* for *Kuala Lumpur* and *JB* for *Johor Bahru* in extracts 64 and 65.

(64) the last time I was in KL it was like . . . more than five years ago
                           {NIECSSE, M8-e:05}

(65) if you count places like . . . er Bintan and JB, yes
                           {NIECSSE, F20-g:14}

In Singapore, all the major expressways and also the names of the universities are referred to by means of initialisms. Figure 4.2 shows a road sign just outside the NTU campus, illustrating initialisms such as these.

Initialisms such as those are common not just in Singapore but throughout South-East Asia, including Hong Kong and the Philippines, though inevitably many of the abbreviations are different. Hong Kong has *ABC* for *American-born Chinese, II* for *illegal immigrant,* and *OSCO* for

Figure 4.2 Initialisms on a road sign just outside the NTU campus.

PIE = Pan-Island Expressway   NTU = Nanyang Technological University
KJE = Kranji Expressway   NIE = National Institute of Education

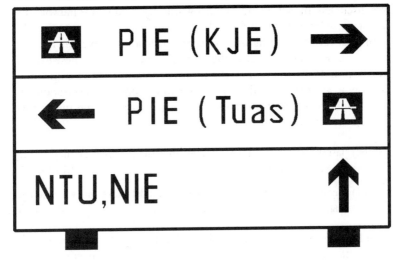

Organised and Serious Crimes Ordinance (Bolton 2003: 212), while the Philippines has *CR* for *Comfort Room, DH* for *Domestic Helper* and *GRO* for *Guest Relations Officer* (Bautista 1997: 61). Of course, use of initialisms is not unique to the region, as throughout the world we have *PC* and *DVD* and even a few cities such as *LA* and countries such as the *UK* and *USA*. However, they do seem particularly common in South-East Asia.

In all varieties of English, the use of initialisms seems to be a modern phenomenon, as it is hard to think of any that existed 100 years ago. Maybe *TV* and *WC* were two of the earliest, though Quinion (2006) observes that *AWOL* (*absent without leave*), which dates from 1918, and *POTUS* (*President of the United States*), which was originally devised by telegraphers in 1879, are probably two of the first real acronyms. It seems that the modern pace of life and the constant drive for efficiency has sanctioned this abbreviated form of writing and speaking, though one wonders whether the impenetrable jargon that sometimes results, especially in Singapore, really is more efficient.

It is also rather ironic that government officials and teachers alike are constantly worried about the use of SMS-style abbreviations such as *ppl* for *people* and *lol* for *laughing out loud* in the writing of young people while at the same time the widespread use of initialisms such as *MOE, HDB, ROM, CPF* and *SAF* is tolerated and even encouraged. One wonders if these two phenomena are not in fact rather similar.

4.11 Shifted meaning in words

In the previous chapter, the idiosyncratic use of *will, would, till* and *already* was discussed. In fact, many English words are used in a somewhat different sense from that found in other varieties of English.

In most varieties of English, *last time* refers to a single event in the past, and *next time* to one instance in the future, but in Singapore these expressions can indicate the past or the future generally. Extract 66 includes the use of *last time* by Hui Min to refer to her previous aspirations for travel, and extract 67 illustrates *next time* to refer to some unspecified time in the future.

(66) last time I would want to go down to Africa . . . yah . . . mmm . . . but I
      don't know about now   {iF13-d:197}

(67) my mum will always says that never mind lah, next time when you get
      married, you'll know how to cook   {iF13-b:40}

In English elsewhere, *bring* usually collocates with *here*, referring to the action of carrying something towards your current location, but in Singapore, *bring* describes taking something or someone along with you regardless of whether that involves coming here or going there. In extract 68, Hui Min uses *bring* to refer to her plans to take her niece and nephews out during the vacation, and similarly extracts 69 and 70 illustrate instances where other varieties of English would use *take* instead of *bring*.

(68) play with my niece and nephews . . . yup . . . bring them out . . . to the
      library   {iF13-b:111}

(69) and we met . . . the local people, and then um . . . yah they bring us
      around   {iF13-c:103}

(70) my dad will have to help up . . . by erm bringing my niece to school in
      the morning   {iF13-l:71}

In most varieties of English, *fetch* refers to the action of going somewhere, picking up something, and bringing it back to the starting place. In contrast, in Singapore *fetch* can describe the action of taking someone to a particular location. In extract 71, Hui Min uses *fetch* in this sense, to refer to a ferry transporting people to two of the small islands to the south of Singapore.

(71) actually the ferry will fetch people to Kusu Island and then to St John
      Island   {iF13-j:265}

In most varieties of English, *stay* refers to temporary residence, but in Singapore English (and indeed in Scottish English) it can refer to living somewhere permanently. Thus in extract 72, Hui Min may have been living in Clementi for a long time, and in extract 73, her relatives have probably lived next door for many years, but in both cases *stay* is used. Similarly, in extract 74 from the NIECSSE data, the speaker uses *stay* even though one imagines that she envisages long-term residence with her husband in their new flat.

(72) though it seems that I I stay in Clementi and then Jurong seems nearer
{iF13-f:184}

(73) my grandmother, my aunt and uncle also stay next door {iF13-k:149}

(74) we are ... buying a new flat ... to ... for me er ... to stay with my husband ... both of us to stay together   {NIECSSE, F25-b:07}

The word *retrenched* is commonly used in Singapore to refer to someone losing their job, where British English might use *laid off* or (more colloquially) *sacked*. The Singapore usage is illustrated in extract 75.

(75) so stayed on ((laugh)) with the company, for another three years, yah, until, until ... it shut down ((laugh)) basically I was retrenched, but before I was retrenched, I actually applied for teaching already
{iF13-e:155}

In Singapore, *marketing* refers to the activity of going to the local market to buy food, rather than working in the marketing division of a company. In extract 76, the speaker is discussing how her dad will help with the household chores now that he has retired.

(76) my dad may help to do, may help in the marketing side, marketing part ... by going to the market to get some ... erm the things that she need lor   {iF13-l:80}

In most of the instances above, it is hard to determine what has caused the shift in meaning. Just occasionally, however, we can observe that the altered meaning is matched by an expression in Chinese, and this might be the source of the shift. For example, *send* is used in Singapore to refer to the action of accompanying a person somewhere, as in extract 77 from the NIECSSE data, and this is rather similar to the Mandarin use of *song* (送) which can refer both to the action of sending a letter and to accompanying someone on a journey. Whether Mandarin or some other variety of Chinese really is the source of this semantic shift with *send* is hard to determine with any degree of certainty.

(77) she ... comes by to ... pick him up and send him elsewhere

{NIECSSE, M4-c:17}

This is just a brief overview of how some words have a shifted meaning in Singapore. In fact, many other words fit into this category, and Brown (1999) provides a more comprehensive list.

4.12 Common use of formal words

Some words which are rather formal or even archaic in British English are used very commonly in Singapore, although there is no shift in meaning. Brown (1999: 195) notes that *sibling* is regarded as formal or scientific in Britain but is common in Singapore. Its usage by Hui Min is illustrated in extracts 78 and 79.

(78) in my family I have my parents, and then um, I have ... myself and four other sibling ... siblings, yup, so I'm the eldest at home

{iF13-k:10}

(79) other than my parents and my siblings, erm, my grandmother, my aunt and uncle also stay next door   {iF13-k:146}

Other examples are to *alight* from a bus or train and *thrice* (Brown 1999: 6, 225). Their usage in Singapore is illustrated in the data from blogs in extracts 80 and 81.

(80) When that train arrived, being kiasu Singaporeans, people rushed forward and pushed their way in without allowing the passengers to alight first.   {Jarhad, 26/6/06}

(81) Eventually I succeeded again but I'm loathe to figure it out thrice after two bouts of frustrating trial and error so I've recorded it down for posterity.   {Beng, 19/6/2006}

Bolton (2003: 214) also mentions the use of archaic words in Hong Kong English, though the words found there are different, with *conservancy*, *subvent* and *teddy boy* still commonly occurring.

4.13 Common phrases

In Singapore, the phrase *as compared to* is often used where something simpler might occur in British or American English. For example, in extract 82, *as compared to* occurs when other varieties of English would be more likely just to use *as*, and in extract 83, *compared to* is used when *than* might be expected.

(82) it's definitely . . . mmm . . . erm . . . not as accessible as compared to the old one {iF13-f:177}

(83) I've never been to New Zealand, maybe that will be a a b- . . . a cheaper . . . place to go compared to Switzerland {iF13-d:287}

4.14 *Actually* and *basically*

Actually and *basically* are both used very regularly in Singapore, and, as discussed in Chapter 2, they are particularly salient because they often carry a sharply rising pitch that we have described as an 'early booster'. In our data, Hui Min uses both these words quite often, with five instances of *actually* in extract 84, and three instances of *basically* in extract 85.

(84) mmm, not really, actually I considered before coming in, into teaching, I mean before erm signing up, I actually thought of being a librarian . . . and teaching is the other option ah, so erm, I actually went for interviews, erm, before I got retrenched, I actually went for interviews with um, National Library Board I mean with um Nanyang Pol-, oh no, Temasek Poly, yah, to work in the library, their libraries, but erm . . . er they actually advised me not to {iF13-e:179}

(85) then there was once I erm . . . almost get drowned, not drowned basically, open inverted comma lah, basically it's that er, but I learnt to use, I learnt to kick, bas- basically the lect- the instructor taught us how to erm do freestyle {iF13-i:111}

Altogether, Hui Min uses nineteen instances of *actually* and thirty-six instances of *basically* in the one hour of her recorded speech. Is this overuse? And is it a feature of Singapore English? We need to keep in mind that British speakers also use both these two words very regularly. Brown (1999: 3) notes that although *actually* is overused in Singapore, this is also common and often criticised in British English, and investigation of the ICE-GB of spoken British English has confirmed that *basically* is also very common in Britain (Doyle and Deterding 2005).

In fact, we should remember that many of the features that we have listed as characteristic of Singapore English are also found in the speech of young British people. In Chapter 2 we discussed the use of glottal stops as well as vocalisation of dark [l]; in Chapter 3, we mentioned the invariant *isn't it* and *right* tags; and in this chapter, we have, considered the regular occurrence of *yah* as well as *actually* and *basically*, but all of these are common in the speech of young people in Britain. Perhaps they constitute part of the speech of young English speakers around the world.

Of course, this does not mean that all aspects of Singapore English are also found in varieties of British English. It is clear that Singapore English has its own style which is quite separate from British varieties, and indeed Singaporeans find some samples of speech by young people from Britain completely incomprehensible (Deterding 2005a). However, we do need to be careful when we describe features of Singapore English, to determine which ones really are special to this variety of the language and which ones are found quite widely elsewhere.

5 History and Current Changes

Chapter 1 included a brief outline of the history of English in Singapore and an overview of language usage in Singapore. In this chapter, we will consider the history a little further, and also discuss variation in Singapore English and the ways in which it has been described. Finally, we will try to evaluate the ways in which Singapore English is currently evolving.

5.1 Recent history of English in Singapore

For most of Singapore's history, English was a minority language, used for official purposes such as in government offices and the law courts and mastered by a small elite, while the majority of the population spoke a variety of Chinese, Malay or Tamil. In 1957, just 1.8 per cent of the population used English as their first language, though of course many others were able to speak it to some extent (Bokhorst-Heng 1998). However, in the past five decades, the government has been actively promoting English, with the result that now virtually all young Singaporeans have a basic competence in the language and many compare well with the best in Britain or America. Furthermore, English is now the first language of a substantial number of people in Singapore. In the 2000 census, 35.8 per cent of Chinese children and 43.6 per cent of Indian children aged between five and fourteen were reported to be speaking English at home, though the language has made smaller inroads in the Malay community, with just 9.4 per cent of Malay children reported as using English as their home language. Indeed, these figures for use of English are increasing fast, as the 35.8 per cent for the Chinese population is an increase from 23.3 per cent in the 1990 census.

The official promotion of English initially met with some resistance, especially from the Chinese community who felt that English was an alien language. This community also felt that the promotion of English undermined a long tradition of excellence in teaching Chinese in schools such

85

as Chinese High and also the recently-established Nanyang University, which was opened in 1956 to offer a Chinese tertiary education for students from the whole South-East Asian region. However, the government persisted for two main reasons: first, English was seen as a vital economic resource, enabling Singapore to find a viable economic role in the modern world in trade and commerce, banking, tourism, education and research; and second, English was seen as a neutral language between the various races, so it could act as a unifying factor allowing for inter-ethnic communication, with no race gaining an unfair advantage (Bokhorst-Heng 1998).

In fact, the promotion of English in Singapore has been so successful that nowadays young people often find that their ethnic language (their 'mother tongue') is the language that they struggle with in school. Initially, when the bilingual policy was implemented, streaming near the end of primary school was done on the basis of grades obtained in four subjects – English, second language, maths and science – and the first two were assigned double weightage. However, it was found that too many bright children were suffering because they scored badly in their second language, so in 1985 the double weightage was scrapped. Similarly, it was noted that many capable students were being prevented from entering university because at the end of their high-school education they were unable to pass the final 'A' level in their second language. Therefore, in 1987 the National University of Singapore implemented a scheme where students could be admitted provisionally and subsequently re-take the second language 'A' level, though they would not be allowed to graduate until they passed it (Gopinathan 1998). Moreover, it is nowadays acceptable for schoolchildren to follow a less challenging curriculum for their second language, in recognition of the fact that many children, even some quite bright ones, are unable to achieve native-like proficiency in two languages. However, a high level of competence in English is increasingly seen as vitally important for all students.

Originally, there were separate streams in schools for English, Chinese, Malay and Tamil, and parents could select which one they wanted for their children. However, in December 1983, the Ministry of Education noted that there were no longer any students enrolled in Malay or Tamil-medium classes, and only 1 per cent of the population were enrolled in Chinese-medium classes, so it was decided that, from 1987 onwards, English would be the primary medium of instruction in all schools, and this policy has remained in place since then (Gopinathan 1998). Furthermore, the option of a Chinese-medium tertiary education was removed in 1981 when Nanyang University was merged with the University of Singapore to create the National University of Singapore, and from then on all university education was in English. When

Nanyang Technological University was founded in 1991 on the former campus of Nanyang University, all classes were also in English, and links with the original Chinese-medium Nanyang University were somewhat tenuous. Although recently some attempts have been made to revive these links, especially with the opening of a Chinese Heritage Centre in the original Nanyang University building, there has never been any suggestion of once more creating a Chinese-medium system of tertiary education. As English has been the basic medium of all education for the past twenty years, and as an increasing number of people speak English at home, it is not surprising that a mature variety of the language has been emerging in Singapore.

Schneider (2003) suggests five stages in the development of varieties of English, from initial foundation in a country where the language was not previously spoken; through stages where usage expands but there continues to be reference to an external norm; and finally, by stage five, a fully mature new variety of English has emerged with its own modes of pronunciation and patterns of use that are free from dependence on external sources of orientation. English in places such as Australia and New Zealand has reached the fifth stage, as the people there no longer make reference to British English for their norms, but Schneider classifies Singapore English as being in the fourth stage, which is characterised by endonormative stabilisation and the gradual adoption and acceptance of local norms. In contrast, English in Malaysia and Philippines has become fossilised in the third stage, partly because in both countries an indigenous language is promoted as the national language, but Schneider envisages that the process in Singapore is likely to proceed through to the fifth stage, so a fully mature, completely self-confident variety of English will eventually emerge.

One of the characteristics of the later stages of Schneider's model, especially the fifth stage, is greater diversification. We will now consider variation in Singapore English and how it has been described.

5.2 Variation in Singapore English

In the pioneering studies of the 1970s and 1980s (for example, Tongue 1979; Platt and Weber 1980), variation in Singapore English was generally described according to the educational level of the speaker: the acrolect was assumed to be spoken by those with a tertiary education, the mesolect was used by those who had completed secondary school, and the basilect was found among speakers with only a primary education or at most one or two years of secondary. However, this approach is rather rigid, as it fails to reflect the fact that most people have the ability to switch between different styles of English according to who they are talking to, where they are, and what they are talking about.

More recently, two alternative approaches have been adopted. Pakir (1991) suggests a model involving expanding triangles of expression, such that the English which is actually used on any one occasion depends on two variables: the education of the speaker and the formality of the situation. This approach emphasises that people select the language they use from a continuum of styles, ranging from formal, educated English to a casual, colloquial style of speech. One problem with this model is it suggests that, although not everyone has access to the most formal variety of English, all speakers do have the ability to use the most colloquial variety. But this is not necessarily true as there are some people, particularly older speakers who were educated in one of the traditional elite English-medium schools, who never slip into the colloquial variety of Singapore English, as it is something they find abhorrent. However, Pakir's model of expanding triangles does represent the flexible usage of English in Singapore quite well.

A slightly different approach to the description of language variation in Singapore is the diglossic one proposed by Gupta (1992a), which suggests that an educated High variety of English is adopted in the most formal situations and a colloquial Low variety (often termed 'Singlish') is used in more casual situations, and people may switch quite abruptly between these two distinct styles of speech. The key issue involves the following question: how distinct are the educated and colloquial varieties of Singapore English? And for speakers who are proficient in both, is it possible to select something half-way between, as would be suggested by the continuum inherent in Pakir's model?

We will now consider how appropriate these two different approaches are for representing the data presented in this book. First, let us consider the speech of Hui Min in the NIECSSE data. Although she is talking to her expatriate academic tutor and presumably using a formal variety of English, there are fifteen instances of null-subject structures and two instances of the discourse particle *ah* during the five minutes of the conversation, even though these two phenomena are listed by Gupta (1994: 10) as diagnostic features for the colloquial variety of the language. This suggests that some colloquial features have crept into the formal speech of this speaker even though she is well educated, which would be a little surprising for a truly diglossic situation in which one might expect clearer separation between the two varieties.

Now let us compare this formal data from Hui Min with her relatively informal speech in the Lim Siew Hwee corpus. A summary of this comparison is shown in Table 5.1.

Table 5.1 Instances of null subjects and discourse particles in the formal and informal data of Hui Min.

Data	Duration (min.)	Null subjects	Discourse particles
Formal	5	15	2
Informal	60	69	79

Table 5.1 shows that there are sixty-nine instances of null-subject structures in the one hour of informal data (1.15 tokens per minute). When compared to the fifteen instances of null-subject structures in the five minutes of the NIECSSE conversation (three tokens per minute), the frequency of this feature is actually substantially lower in the informal data, which is rather unexpected. Perhaps null-subject structures are inevitably more common in the dialogue that constitutes the NIECSSE data than in the informal recording which is basically just an extended monologue with occasional questions from the interviewer to encourage her to continue. So maybe for these two sources of data, comparison of the occurrence of null subjects is not really valid.

Table 5.1 also shows that there are seventy-nine instances of discourse particles in the one hour of the informal data (1.3 tokens per minute), and this is rather more frequent than the two tokens in five minutes of the more formal NIECSSE data (0.4 tokens per minute). This is more as we might predict and it does suggest a shift in styles between the two recordings.

Although on the basis of the occurrence of discourse particles we may conclude that the informal data does represent a more colloquial style of speech, it should still be described as reasonably educated Singapore English and it does not resemble truly colloquial Singapore English, especially as standard subject-verb agreement is mostly maintained, there are not too many instances of omission of the copula verb *be*, and borrowings from local languages are almost entirely absent (with just two instances of Mandarin words when a suitable English word was not immediately available to the speaker). So a comparison between the formal speech in the NIECSSE data and the relatively informal conversation with her friend seems to suggest a shift along a continuum of styles rather than a sharp switch between a High and a Low variety. Hui Min probably has a much more colloquial variety of English that she may use in truly casual situations when she is not being recorded, though obtaining data for this is not easy. In conclusion, Pakir's model of expanding triangles seems to be more applicable for the description of these two kinds of data.

However, this does not mean that Gupta's diglossic model is without merit, as it does accurately describe the very frequent instances when speakers make a clear, abrupt switch between two quite distinct varieties of English. In fact, in educational policy, the diglossic model represents what many would regard as the goal, as a colloquial variety of English can be tolerated and even celebrated so long as all pupils develop the ability to switch to use of standard English when that is appropriate, and teachers often seek to encourage this kind of clear shift according to circumstances. If this becomes established as normal behaviour, we should not worry too much if pupils use a colloquial variety of the language among themselves as long as teachers always promote standard English in the classroom and ensure that their pupils develop the ability to communicate reasonably proficiently in this more formal variety.

We must acknowledge, however, that encouragement of such a clear diglossic separation of the two varieties might be a bit idealistic, as there is widespread concern, especially among government circles, about whether less capable students really can develop two such clearly defined varieties of English, especially when they have to study a second language as well. We will now consider the current attitudes of the government to the use of English in Singapore.

5.3 Government attitudes towards Singapore English

In contrast to some countries, such as Britain or the USA, where the governments have traditionally had a fairly *laissez-faire* approach to language use, the government of Singapore has always paid close attention to language issues. Even top ministers, including the prime minister, have been keenly involved in all matters regarding language policy, including the original selection of the four official languages and the promotion of Mandarin at the expense of the Chinese dialects (Bokhorst-Heng 1998).

In recent years, the emergence and widespread use of a colloquial variety of English, which many young speakers regard as 'cool', has become a matter of some concern to the government. In his 1999 National Day Rally, Prime Minister Goh Chok Tong observed:

> If we carry on using Singlish, the logical final outcome is that we, too, will develop our own type of pidgin English, spoken by only 3 million Singaporeans, which the rest of the world will find quaint but incomprehensible. We are already there. Do we want to go the whole way? (*The Straits Times*, 23 August 1999, quoted in Rubdy 2001: 345)

And former Prime Minister Lee Kuan Yew expressed his aversion to Singlish even more strongly, asserting that it constitutes a serious handicap that is harming the economic development of Singapore.

One way devised by the government to counter the spread of Singlish is by means of the Speak Good English Movement (SGEM) which was launched in April 2000. Some recent activities promoted by SGEM include regular newspaper columns that discuss 'correct' English usage and highlight instances of 'broken' English, and workshops run in regional libraries that teach participants to read phonetic symbols with the aim of enabling them to check the standard pronunciation of words in a dictionary. Rubdy (2001) compares SGEM to the on-going annual Speak Mandarin Campaign, for both seek, primarily for economic reasons, to encourage the use of a standard variety of a major international language, since it is considered essential for economic survival that Singaporeans can communicate with businessmen and visitors both from the West and from China.

The Speak Mandarin Campaign has been extraordinarily successful, to the extent that Mandarin Chinese, a language that almost nobody in Singapore spoke as a home language thirty years ago, is now the common language among young Chinese Singaporeans. Will the Speak Good English Movement be equally effective? Given the track record of the government in persuading the people of Singapore to change their habits, not just in the use of language but also in other areas such as flushing public toilets and not chewing gum, it is quite possible that the popular use of Singlish will indeed be eliminated. Only time will tell.

5.4 Popular attitudes towards Singapore English

In addition to the concerns of government ministers about the ways English is used in Singapore, there is a keen interest in language from the general public. Almost every day there are letters in the *The Straits Times* discussing English usage, most of them complaining about falling standards but a few offering a dissenting voice and insisting that Singlish is a valued badge of identity for Singaporeans.

Have standards really been falling? Clearly, use of English in Singapore is much more widespread nowadays than it used to be, and it makes no sense to compare the English of a small, well educated elite in the past with the language used by the bulk of the population today, so any perception of falling standards based on that kind of comparison is flawed. In fact, figures from the Ministry of Education show that exam results in English language have been gradually but consistently improving among the population in Singapore as a whole. But still the perception remains that standards are falling.

Concerns about the degeneration of English are nothing new. In 1710, Jonathan Swift wrote a scathing attack on the standard of English (Aitchison 2001: 8), but somehow, through the intervening three centuries, we have still (usually) continued to understand each other. In 1797 John Walker complained about the disgusting use of [ɑː] in words such as *fast* and *bath*, and in 1868 Thomas Hood fulminated about the loss of [r] resulting in such atrocities as *morn* rhyming with *dawn* (Mugglestone 2003: 79, 88), but in time both of these new-fangled modes of speaking became the norm in much of Britain without the whole fabric of society collapsing.

Or maybe things are different today. Perhaps standards really are falling, partly because the proliferation of SMS shorthand in the modern age has corrupted the way young people write, and maybe in Singapore the popularity of a colloquial variety of English really does undermine the ability of most people to be understood in the rest of the world.

In this book, we have described the English of one educated speaker in some detail. It is hoped that readers will be able to listen to the data and judge for themselves whether it is intelligible to people around the world. Kirkpatrick and Saunders (2005) investigated something similar when they played recordings of six different speakers from the NIECSSE data to students in Australia, and they found that most of their students were able to understand the speech reasonably well, though people from some parts of Asia such as China, Taiwan, Japan, Iraq and Bhutan had a little more difficulty.

Of course, the data from Hui Min and also the NIECSSE data are not representative of all speakers in Singapore, and it is certainly true that we could offer many samples of speech that would be largely incomprehensible for people from elsewhere, so it must be acknowledged that plenty of young people in Singapore continue to have a poor command of the language. However, if listeners agree that the speech of Hui Min is clear and articulate even though it includes so many features of Singapore English, maybe we really do not have so much to fear about falling standards, at least for trainee teachers. And indeed, there are many features of the speech discussed here that are distinctly Singaporean but do not interfere in any way with intelligibility. In conclusion, then, it is quite possible to sound Singaporean but still be easily understood in the rest of the world, and it seems that a mature variety of educated Singapore English is indeed emerging.

6 Annotated Bibliography

In this bibliography, we will first survey the general books on Singapore English and then consider some specific books and key papers in each area.

6.1 General books on Singapore English

Tongue (1979) is the first substantial work on English in Singapore. It continues to make a lot of sense even after all these years, and it is still well worth reading. Platt and Weber (1980) is also an important early work on Singapore English. More recently, Gupta (1994) is an influential book that documents in some detail the language development among children in Singapore as well as providing a general overview of Singapore English. Brown (1999) offers a comprehensive and authoritative list of words and features that occur in Singapore English, and it is an essential reference work for anyone interested in the subject. Low and Brown (2005) is an introductory textbook on the history, sociology, grammar and phonetics of Singapore English which is a valuable resource for all scholars as it covers a wide range of topics in some detail.

There are a number of edited volumes that offer collections of articles on Singapore English. Crewe (1997) contains some classic early papers on Singapore English. More recently, Foley et al. (1998) is a valuable set of overviews of various aspects of English in Singapore, though it is a pity nobody took on the role of editing the volume to ensure greater consistency between the different contributions. Gopinathan et al. (1998) is a collection of important articles about various facets of language use in Singapore, particularly sociolinguistic issues and summaries of shifts in official policy. Ooi (2001) is a recent volume of papers on the English of Singapore and Malaysia, many of which include useful new data. Finally Lim (2004) offers some substantial analyses of the pronunciation and grammar of Singapore English based on a corpus collected at NUS, though the value of this work would be enhanced if the corpus were made more widely available.

A series of books published by the Singapore Association for Applied Linguistics (SAAL) offers articles on a range of topics, and these provide excellent resources into many aspects of Singapore English. In particular, Pakir (1993) and Teng and Ho (1995) are collections of conference papers from the early 1990s. Other titles in this SAAL series on more restricted topics are mentioned below.

Two web-based bibliographies on Singapore English are http://davidd.myplace.nie.edu.sg/books/singapore-english-bibliography.htm and http://www.leeds.ac.uk/english/staff/afg/singeb2.html.

6.2 History, sociolinguistics and language policy

For population data, including languages used at home, see Singapore Department of Statistics (2006). For a history of English in Singapore, see Gupta (1994), which also considers the historical influence of Indians in Singapore (1994: 39). For a discussion of official shifts in policy towards the use of English in schools and also matters concerning the Speak Mandarin Campaign, see Gopinathan (1998), and for an overview of changes in language policy in Singapore, see Bokhorst-Heng (1998). For a discussion of the Speak Good English Movement, including a thoughtful comparison with the Speak Mandarin Campaign, see Rubdy (2001). For a discussion of language use in the Tamil community in Singapore, see Saravanan (1998).

Gupta (1992a) presents the diglossic nature of style switching in Singapore English, and Gupta (1994) shows how children develop the ability to switch between a High and a Low variety of the language. Pakir (1991) offers an alternative analysis based on expanding triangles of English expression. Low and Brown (2005: 36–40) provides a comparison of these two approaches.

6.3 Phonetics and phonology

Tongue (1979: ch. 1) provides an early overview of the pronunciation of Singapore English. More recent summaries can be found in Bao (1998), Deterding and Poedjosoedarmo (1998: ch. 17), Low et al. (2002), Lim (2004), Wee (2004a), Low and Brown (2005: chs 8–12) and Brown and Deterding (2005).

For a discussion of vowel distinctions in Singapore English, see Brown (1988b) or Low et al. (2002). For recent measurements of the quality of vowels, see Deterding (2003a) and Deterding (2005b).

Deterding (1994) describes the intonation of Singapore English, and Goh (2000) does the same within a discourse intonation framework. Goh

(2005) presents an attempt to transcribe data from the NIECSSE corpus using the British model of discourse intonation, and Levis (2005) discusses differences between the intonation of Singapore and American English. Brown et al. (2000), from the SAAL series, is a collection of research papers on the pronunciation of Singapore English, and it includes a comprehensive bibliography (Brown 2000). Deterding et al. (2005) is a further collection of phonetic research papers all of which are based on analysis of data in the NIECSSE corpus, a copy of which is provided with the book; the final chapter (Brown 2005) of the collection is an updated bibliography of works on pronunciation in Singapore.

6.4 Morphology and syntax

Tongue (1979: ch. 2) provides an early overview of many grammatical issues in Singapore English. More recent summaries can be found in Alsagoff and Ho (1998), Deterding and Poedjosoedarmo (2001: ch. 19), Wee (2004b) and Low and Brown (2005: ch. 7).

For detailed analysis of tense usage, see Ho and Platt (1993). Even if the precise results for the occurrence of past tense verbs might be questioned, this book still offers a valuable snapshot of verb usage in Singapore. For use of the present tense in narratives, *will* to refer to regular events, and *would* for tentative usage, see Deterding (2003b). For other issues regarding verbs, see Alsagoff (2001) or Fong (2004).

Deterding et al. (2003) is a recent collection of research papers on grammar, of which half are descriptive and half focus on teaching. In the last chapter of the collection, Brown (2003) offers a comprehensive bibliography of works on the grammar of Singapore English.

6.5 Discourse and lexis

Tongue (1979: ch. 3) provides a collection of words with shifted meanings in Singapore English, though some of the entries are now a little dated. More recently, Brown (1999) offers a substantial list of borrowings and lexical items with shifted meaning, with attempts to illustrate how each item is used. Wee (1998) offers an overview of lexical issues in Singapore English, as does Low and Brown (2005: ch. 6).

For recent discussions of the use of discourse particles, see Low and Deterding (2003), Wee (2004c), or Low and Brown (2005: 175–80).

6.6 References

Aitchison, Jean (2001), *Language Change: Progress or Decline*, 3rd edn, Cambridge: Cambridge University Press.

Alsagoff, Lubna (1992), 'Topic in Malay: The other subject', unpublished PhD thesis, Stanford University.

Alsagoff, Lubna (1995), 'Colloquial Singapore English: the relative clause construction', in Teng and Ho (eds) (1995), pp. 77–87.

Alsagoff, Lubna (2001), 'Tense and aspect in Singapore English', in Ooi (ed.) (2001), pp. 79–88.

Alsagoff, Lubna and Ho Chee Lick (1998), 'The grammar of Singapore English', in Foley et al. (eds) (1998), pp. 127–51.

Ansaldo, Umberto (2004), 'The evolution of Singapore English: finding the matrix', in Lim (ed.) (2004), pp. 127–49.

Bao Zhiming (1995), '*Already* in Singapore English', *World Englishes*, 14(2), 181–8.

Bao Zhiming (1998), 'The sounds of Singapore English', in Foley et al. (eds) (1998), pp. 152–74.

Bao Zhiming (2001), 'The origins of empty categories in Singapore English', *Journal of Pidgin and Creole Languages*, 16(2), 275–301.

Bao Zhiming and Wee, Lionel (1998), '*Until* in Singapore English', *World Englishes*, 17(1), 31–44.

Baskaran, Loga (2004a), 'Malaysian English: phonology', in Schneider et al. (eds) (2004), pp. 1034–46.

Baskaran, Loga (2004b), 'Malaysian English: morphology and syntax', in Kortmann et al. (eds) (2004), pp. 1073–85.

Bautista, Maria Lourdes S. (1997), 'The lexicon of Philippine English', in Maria Lourdes S. Bautista (ed.), *English is an Asian Language. Proceedings of the Conference Held in Manila on August 2–3 1996*, Macquarie University, Australia: The Macquarie Library Pty Ltd, pp. 49–72.

Bell, Roger and Ser Peng Quee, Larry (1983), ' "Today la?" "Tomorrow lah!" The LA particle in Singapore English', *RELC Journal*, 14(2), 1–18.

Bodman, Nicholas (1955), *Spoken Amoy Hokkien*, Kuala Lumpur: Government of the Federation of Malaya.

Boersma, Paul and Weenink, David (2005), 'Praat: doing phonetics by computer', accessed on 11 May 2005 at <http://www.fon.hum.uva.nl/praat/>.

Bokhorst-Heng, Wendy (1998), 'Language planning and management in Singapore', in Foley et al. (eds) (1998), pp. 287–309.

Bolton, Kingsley (2003), *Chinese Englishes: A Sociolinguistic History*, Cambridge: Cambridge University Press.

Brown, Adam (1988a), 'The staccato effect in the pronunciation of English in Malaysia and Singapore', in Foley (ed.) (1988), pp. 115–28.

Brown, Adam (1988b), 'Vowel differences between Received Pronunciation and the English of Malaysia and Singapore: which ones really matter?', in Foley (ed.) (1988), pp. 129–47.

Brown, Adam (1999), *Singapore English in a Nutshell: An Alphabetical Description of its Features*, Singapore: Federal Publications.

Brown, Adam (2000), 'Bibliography on Singapore English pronunciation', in Brown et al. (eds) (2000), pp. 133–43.

Brown, Adam (2003), 'A bibliography on Singapore English grammar', in Deterding et al. (eds) (2003), pp. 152–65.

Brown, Adam (2005), 'A bibliography on Singapore English pronunciation', in Deterding et al. (eds) (2005), pp. 184–202.

Brown, Adam and Deterding, David (2005), 'A checklist of Singapore English pronunciation features', in Deterding et al. (eds) (2005), pp. 7–13.

Brown, Adam, Deterding, David and Low Ee Ling (eds) (2000), *The English Language in Singapore: Research on Pronunciation*, Singapore: Singapore Association for Applied Linguistics.

Carter, Ronald and McCarthy, Michael (2006), *Cambridge Grammar of English: A Comprehensive Guide*, Cambridge: Cambridge University Press.

Crewe, William (ed.) (1977), *The English Language in Singapore*, Singapore: Eastern Universities Press.

Cruttenden, Alan (1997), *Intonation*, 2nd edn, Cambridge: Cambridge University Press.

Cruttenden, Alan (2001), *Gimson's Pronunciation of English*, 6th edn, London: Arnold.

Crystal, David (2003), *English as a Global Language*, 2nd edn, Cambridge: Cambridge University Press.

Date, Tamikazu (2005), 'The intelligibility of Singapore English from a Japanese perspective', in Deterding et al. (eds) (2005), pp. 173–83.

Deterding, David (1994), 'The intonation of Singapore English', *Journal of the International Phonetic Association*, 24(2), 61–72.

Deterding, David (1997), 'The formants of monophthong vowels in Standard Southern British English Pronunciation', *Journal of the International Phonetic Association*, 27, 47–55.

Deterding, David (2000), 'Measurements of the /eɪ/ and /əʊ/ vowels of young English speakers in Singapore', in Brown et al. (eds) (2000), pp. 93–9.

Deterding, David (2001), 'The measurement of rhythm: a comparison of Singapore and British English', *Journal of Phonetics*, 29(2), 217–30.

Deterding, David (2003a), 'An instrumental study of the monophthong vowels of Singapore English', *English World Wide*, 24(1), 1–16.

Deterding, David (2003b), 'Tenses and *will/would* in a corpus of Singapore English', in Deterding et al. (eds) (2003), pp. 31–8.

Deterding, David (2005a), 'Listening to Estuary English in Singapore', *TESOL Quarterly*, 39(3), 425–40.

Deterding, David (2005b), 'Emergent patterns in the vowels of Singapore English', *English World-Wide*, 26(2), 179–97.

Deterding, David (2006a), 'The pronunciation of English by speakers from China', *English World-Wide*, 27(2), 175–98.

Deterding, David (2006b), 'Deletion of final /t/ and /d/ in BBC English: implications for teachers in Singapore', *STETS Language & Communication Review*, 5(1), 21–3.

Deterding, David, Brown, Adam and Low Ee Ling (eds) (2005), *English in Singapore: Phonetic Research on a Corpus*, Singapore: McGraw-Hill Education (Asia).

Deterding, David and Kirkpatrick, Andy (2006), 'Emerging South-East Asian Englishes and intelligibility', *World Englishes*, 25(3/4), pp. 391–409.

Deterding, David and Lim Siew Hwee (2005), 'The Lim Siew Hwee Corpus of Informal Singapore Speech', accessed on 23 January 2006 at <http:// videoweb.nie.edu.sg/phonetic/lim-siew-hwee-corpus/index.htm>.

Deterding, David and Low Ee Ling (2003), 'A corpus-based description of particles in spoken Singapore English', in Deterding et al. (eds) (2003), pp. 58–66.

Deterding, David and Low Ee Ling (2005), 'The NIE Corpus of Spoken Singapore English', in Deterding et al. (eds) (2005), pp. 1–6.

Deterding, David, Low Ee Ling and Brown, Adam (eds) (2003), *English in Singapore: Research on Grammar*, Singapore: McGraw-Hill Education (Asia).

Deterding, David and Poedjosoedarmo, Gloria (1998), *The Sounds of English: Phonetics and Phonology for English Teachers in Southeast Asia*, Singapore: Prentice-Hall.

Deterding, David and Poedjosoedarmo, Gloria (2000), 'To what extent can the ethnic group of Singaporeans be identified by their speech?', in Brown et al. (eds) (2000), pp. 1–8.

Deterding, David and Poedjosoedarmo, Gloria (2001), *The Grammar of English: Morphology and Syntax for English Teachers in Southeast Asia*, Singapore: Prentice-Hall.

Doyle, Paul and Deterding, David (2005), 'A corpus-based study of *actually* and *basically* in Singapore English', paper presented at 40th International RELC Seminar, Singapore, 18–20 April 2005.

Foley, Joseph (ed.) (1988), *New Englishes: The Case of Singapore*, Singapore: Singapore University Press.

Foley, J. A, Kandiah, T., Bao Zhiming, Gupta, A. F., Alsagoff, L., Ho Chee Lick, Wee, L., Talib, I. S. and Bokhorst-Heng, W. (eds) (1998), *English in New Cultural Contexts*, Singapore: Singapore Institute of Management/Oxford University Press.

Fong, Vivienne (2004), 'The verbal cluster', in Lim (ed.) (2004), pp. 75–104.

Foulkes, Paul and Docherty, Gerard J. (2000), 'Another chapter in the story of /r/: "Labiodental" variants in British English', *Journal of Sociolinguistics*, 4(1), 30–59.

Goh, Christine C. M. (2000), 'A discourse approach to the description of intonation in Singapore English', in Brown et al. (eds) (2000), pp. 35–45.

Goh, Christine C. M. (2005), 'Discourse intonation variants in the speech of educated Singaporeans', in Deterding et al. (eds) (2005), pp. 104–14.

Gopinathan, S. (1998), 'Language policy changes, 1979–1997: politics and pedagogy', in Gopinathan et al. (eds) (1998) pp. 19–44.

Gopinathan, S., Pakir, Anne, Ho Wah Kam and Saravanan, Vanithamani (eds)

(1998), *Language, Society and Education in Singapore*, 2nd edn, Singapore: Times Academic Press.

Gupta, Anthea Fraser (1992a), 'Contact features of Singapore Colloquial English', in Kingsley Bolton and Helen Kwok (eds), *Sociolinguistics Today: International Perspectives*, London and New York: Routledge, pp. 323–45.

Gupta, Anthea Fraser (1992b), 'The pragmatic particles of Singapore Colloquial English', *Journal of Pragmatics*, 18, 31–57.

Gupta, Anthea Fraser (1994), *The Step-Tongue: Children's English in Singapore*, Clevedon, UK: Multimedia Matters.

Gupta, Anthea Fraser (2006), 'Singlish on the Web', in Azirah Hasim and Norizah Hassan (eds), *Varieties of English in Southeast Asia and Beyond*, Kuala Lumpur: University of Malaya Press, pp. 19–37.

Gut, Ulrike (2005), 'The realisation of final plosives in Singapore English: phonological rules and ethnic differences', in Deterding et al. (eds) (2005), pp. 14–25.

Heng Mui Gek and Deterding, David (2005), 'Reduced vowels in conversational Singapore English', in Deterding et al. (eds) (2005), pp. 54–63.

Ho Mian Lian and Platt, John (1993), *Dynamics of a Contact Continuum: Singapore English*, Oxford: Clarendon Press.

Hung, Tony (2000), 'Towards a phonology of Hong Kong English', *World Englishes*, 19, 337–56.

Kachru, Braj B. (2005), *Asian Englishes: Beyond the Canon*, Hong Kong: Hong Kong University Press.

Kirkpatrick, Andy and Saunders, Neville (2005), 'The intelligibility of Singaporean English: a case study in an Australian university', in Deterding et al. (eds) (2005), pp. 153–62.

Kortmann, Bernd, Burridge, Kate, Mesthrie, Rajend, Schneider, Edgar W. and Upton, Clive (eds) (2004), *A Handbook of Varieties of English. Volume 2: Morphology and Syntax*, Berlin: Mouton de Gruyter.

Kwan-Terry, Anna (1978), 'The meaning and the source of the "la" and the "what" particles in Singapore English', *RELC Journal*, 9(2), 22–36.

Kwek, Geraldine (2005), 'The Labiodental /r/ in Standard Singapore English', unpublished English Language Honours Academic Exercise, National Institute of Education, Singapore.

Labov, William (1966), *The Social Stratification of English in New York City*, Washington, DC: Center for Applied Linguistics.

Lee Ee May and Lim, Lisa (2000), 'Diphthongs in Singaporean English: their realisation across different formality levels and some attitudes of listeners towards them', in Brown et al. (eds) (2000), pp. 100–11.

Levis, John M. (2005), 'Prominence in Singapore and American English: evidence from reading aloud', in Deterding et al. (eds) (2005), pp. 86–94.

Li, Charles N. and Thompson, Sandra A. (1981), *Mandarin Chinese: A Functional Reference Grammar*, Berkeley: University of California Press.

Liaw Yock Fang (1999), *Malay Grammar Made Easy*, Singapore: Times Books.

Lim, Gerard (2001), 'Till divorce do us part: the case of Singaporean and Malaysian English', in Ooi (ed.) (2001), pp. 125–39.

Lim, Lisa (2000), 'Ethnic group differences aligned? Intonation patterns of

Chinese, Indian and Malay Singaporean English', in Brown et al. (eds) (2000), pp. 10–21.

Lim, Lisa (2004), 'Sounding Singaporean', in Lim (ed.) (2004), pp. 19–56.

Lim, Lisa (ed.) (2004), *Singapore English: A Grammatical Description*, Amsterdam: John Benjamins.

Lim Siew Hwee (2003), 'Extra final consonants in Educated Singapore English', National Institute of Education English Language Honours Academic Exercise.

Lim Siew Hwee and Deterding, David (2005), 'Added final plosives in Singapore English', in Deterding et al. (eds) (2005), pp. 37–42.

Lim Siew Siew and Low Ee Ling (2005), 'Triphthongs in Singapore English', in Deterding et al. (eds) (2005), pp. 64–73.

Loke Kit Ken and Low, Johna M. Y. (1988), 'A proposed descriptive framework for the pragmatic meanings of the particle LA in colloquial Singaporean English', *Asian-Pacific Papers: Applied Linguistics of Australia Occasional Papers*, 2, 150–61.

Low Ee Ling (2000), 'A comparison of the pitch range of Singapore English and British English speakers', in Brown et al. (eds) (2000), pp. 46–52.

Low Ee Ling and Brown, Adam (2005), *English in Singapore: An Introduction*, Singapore: McGraw-Hill.

Low Ee Ling and Deterding, David (2003), 'A corpus-based description of particles in spoken Singapore English', in Deterding et al. (eds) (2003), pp. 58–66.

Low Ee Ling, Deterding, David and Brown, Adam (2002), 'The nature and importance of pronunciation features in Singapore English', in Low Ee Ling and Teng Su Ching (eds), *The Teaching and Use of Standard English*, Singapore: Singapore Association for Applied Linguistics, pp. 33–44.

Low Ee Ling, Grabe, Esther and Nolan, Francis (2000), 'Quantitative characterisations of speech rhythm: syllable-timing in Singapore English', *Language and Speech*, 43, 377–401.

Morais, Elaine (2001), 'Lectal varieties of Malaysian English', in Ooi (ed.) (2001), pp. 33–52.

Moorthy, Shanti Marion and Deterding, David (2000), 'Three or tree? Dental fricatives in the speech of educated Singaporeans', in Brown et al. (eds) (2000), pp. 76–83.

Mossop, Jonathan (1996), 'Some phonological features of Brunei English', in Peter W. Martin, Conrad Ozóg and Gloria Poedjosoedarmo (eds), *Language Use and Language Change in Brunei Darussalam*, Athens, Ohio: Ohio University Centre for International Studies, pp. 189–208.

Mugglestone, Lynda (2003), *Talking Proper: The Rise of Accent as Social Symbol*, 2nd edn, Oxford: Oxford University Press.

Nelson, Gerald, Wallis, Sean and Aarts, Bas (2002), *Exploring Natural Language: Working with the British Component of the International Corpus of English*, Amsterdam: John Benjamins.

Newbrook, Mark (2003), 'Features of the relative clause in Singapore English', in Deterding et al. (eds) (2003), pp. 67–76.

Ooi, Vincent B. Y. (ed.) (2001), *Evolving Identities: The English Language in Singapore and Malaysia*, Singapore: Times Academic.

Pakir, Anne (1991), 'The range and depth of English-knowing bilinguals in Singapore', *World Englishes,* 10(2), 167–79.

Pakir, Anne (ed.) (1993), *The English Language in Singapore: Standards and Norms,* Singapore: Singapore Association for Applied Linguistics.

Platt, John and Weber, Heidi (1980), *English in Singapore and Malaysia: Status, Functions, Features,* Singapore: Oxford University Press.

Poedjosoedarmo, Gloria (2000a), 'Influences of Malay on the written English of university students in Singapore', in Adam Brown (ed.), *English in Southeast Asia 99. Proceedings of the Fourth 'English in Southeast Asia' conference,* Singapore: National Institute of Education, pp. 210–19.

Poedjosoedarmo, Gloria (2000b), 'The media as a model and source of innovation in the development of Singapore Standard English', in Brown et al. (eds) (2000), pp. 112–20.

Quinion, Michael (2006), 'Weird words: POTUS', *WorldWideWords,* 497, 22 July 2006, accessed on 23 July 2006 at <http://www.worldwidewords.org/nl/zevs.htm>.

Radford, Andrew (1997), *Syntactic Theory and the Structure of English: A Minimalist Approach,* Cambridge: Cambridge University Press.

Richards, Jack C. and Tay, Mary W. J. (1977), 'The *la* particle in Singapore English', in Crewe (ed.) (1977), pp. 141–56.

Rubdy, Rani (2001), 'Creative destruction: Singapore English's Speak Good English movement', *World Englishes,* 20(3), 341–55.

Saravanan, Vanithamani (1998), 'Language maintenance and language shift in the Tamil-English community', in Gopinathan et al. (eds) (1998), pp. 155–78.

Schneider, Edgar W. (2003), 'The dynamics of New Englishes: from identity construction to dialect birth', *Language,* 79, 233–81.

Schneider, Edgar W., Burridge, Kate, Kortmann, Bernd, Mesthrie, Rajend, and Upton, Clive (eds) (2004), *A Handbook of Varieties of English. Volume 1: Phonology,* Berlin: Mouton de Gruyter.

Setter, Jane and Deterding, David (2003), 'Extra final consonants in the English of Hong Kong and Singapore', paper presented at the International Congress of Phonetic Sciences, Barcelona, 2003.

Singapore Department of Statistics (2006), 'Statistics Singapore – KeyStats', accessed on 9 July 2006 at <http://www.singstat.gov.sg/keystats/annual/indicators.html>.

Stenström, Anna-Brita, Anderson, Gisle and Hasund, Ingrid Kristine (2002), *Trends in Teenage Talk: Corpus Compilation, Analysis and Findings,* Amsterdam/Philadelphia: John Benjamins.

Suzanna binte Hashim and Brown, Adam (2000), 'The [e] and [æ] vowels in Singapore English', in Brown et al. (eds) (2000), pp. 84–92.

Taiwan Language Committee (2005), *Elementary Taiwanese for Foreigners,* Taipei: Kaito Publishing Company.

Tan, Kah Keong (2005), 'Vocalisation of /l/ in Singapore English', in Deterding et al. (eds) (2005), pp. 43–53.

Tan, Ludwig (2003), 'Topic Prominence and null arguments in Singapore Colloquial English', in Deterding et al. (eds) (2003), pp. 1–10.

Tan, Ludwig (2007), 'Null arguments in Singapore Colloquial English', unpublished PhD thesis, Cambridge University Department of Linguistics.

Tay Wan Joo, Mary (1982), 'The phonology of educated Singapore English', *English World-Wide*, 3(2), 135–45.

Tayao, Ma Lourdes G. (2004), 'Philippine English: phonology', in Schneider et al. (eds) (2004), pp. 1047–59.

Teng Su Ching and Ho Mian Lian (eds) (1995), *The English Language in Singapore: Implications for Teaching*, Singapore: Singapore Association for Applied Linguistics.

Teoh Boon Seng, Lim Beng Soon and Lee Liang Hye (2003), 'A study of Penang Peranakan Hokkien', *Journal of Modern Languages*, Faculty of Languages and Linguistics, University of Malaya, 15, 169–90.

Tong, Keith S. T. and James, Gregory (1994), *Colloquial Cantonese*, London and New York: Routledge.

Tongue, R. K. (1979), *The English of Singapore and Malaysia*, 2nd edn, Singapore: Eastern Universities Press.

Wee, Lionel (1998), 'The lexis of Singapore English', in Foley et al. (eds) (1998), pp. 175–200.

Wee, Lionel (2004a), 'Singapore English: Phonology', in Schneider et al. (eds) (2004), pp. 1017–33.

Wee, Lionel (2004b), 'Singapore English: morphology and syntax', in Kortmann et al. (eds) (2004), pp. 1058–72.

Wee, Lionel (2004c), 'Reduplication and discourse particles', in Lim (ed.) (2004), pp. 105–26.

Wee, Lionel and Ansaldo, Umberto (2004), 'Nouns and noun phrases', in Lim (ed.) (2004), pp. 57–74.

Wells, J. C. (1982), *Accents of English*, Cambridge: Cambridge University Press.

Wells, J. C. (2000), *Longman Pronunciation Dictionary*, Harlow: Longman.

Blogs

(All blogs were accessed using the Technorati search engine: http://technorati.com/.)

Anikin Goh (4/1/06), accessed on 16 June 2006 at <http://anikingmg.blogspot.com/2006/01/open-thoughts.html>

Beng (19/6/06), accessed on 30 June 2006 at <http://me.benghee.net/2006/06/19/perhaps-pointless-palindrome-ponderings/>

Defy Angel (16/6/06), accessed on 16 June 2006 at <http://defy_angel.blogspot.com/2006/06/all-packed-and-ready-to-go.html>

Divya (25/6/06), accessed on 26 June 2006 at <http://divyamenon.blogs.friendster.com/divs/2006/06/polite_singapor.html>

Gabe (24/6/06), accessed on 24 June 2006 at <http://theobskure.org/home/>

gaussito (24/6/06), accessed on 5 July 2006 at <http://yesimtakingabreak.blogspot.com/>

Jarhad (26/6/06), accessed on 1 July 2006 at <http://www.freewebs.com/jarhad/myblog.htm?blogentryid=603374>

Jing (5/5/06), accessed on 16 June 2006 at <http://titanic-unsinkable. blog-spot.com/2005/05/wonderful-week.html>

Ning (15/6/06), accessed on 24 June 2006 at <http://same-old-brand-new-me.blogspot.com/2006/06/nowadays-like-very-heng-go-anywhere.html>

Ryan (4/6/06), accessed on 16 June 2006 at <http://ryantwz.blogspot.com/2006/06/journey-to-west.html>

Shuyi (12/6/06), accessed on 26 June 2006 at <http://everydaymumblings. blogspot.com/2006/06/day-9.html>

shygal001 (22/6/06), accessed on 24 June 2006 at <http://blushingqueen. blogspot.com/2006/06/mmvds-have-been-tagged-by-masbokz.html>

SK (7/5/06), accessed on 15 June 2006 at <http://adidask57.blogspot.com/2006/05/untitled.html>

Timmy Goh (11/6/06), accessed on 5 July at <http://kaiyiz.blogspot.com/2006/06/singapore-idols-puh-eeeee.html>

Timothy Tan (26/11/05), accessed on 16 June 2006 at <http://lordaero. blogspot.com/2005/11/ilfords-kodachromes-porst.html>

Vicky (8/6/06), accessed on 15 June 2006 at <http://vickychen.wordpress. com/2006/06/08/my-problems/>

WseeH (2/6/06), accessed on 1 July 2006 at <http://6e-essaysblog. blog-spot.com/>

Yuhui Han (23/5/06), accessed on 26 June 2006 at <http://psychedelicflux. spaces.msn.com/>

7 Texts: Transcripts for the Data of Hui Min

Transcription conventions

Int	the speech of the interviewer
HM	the speech of Hui Min
50	the time in seconds from the start of the file is shown in the left-hand column
((laughs))	non-linguistic sound
. . .	pause
s-	incomplete word

(The first draft of the transcripts for the data of Hui Min was completed by Ludwig Tan.)

iF13-a

	Int	OK, so what did you do last weekend?
	HM	Last weekend, erm, I went to . . . I did quite a few things during the weekends, firstly I went back to the primary school that I . . . taught for the past three weeks . . . to settle some s- . . . some things with the . . . the teachers there . . . er and to finish up . . . marking also . . . erm after that I came back to NIE to do . . . some library research . . . till about three-thirty . . . three-thirty, yah . . . then later on in the evening . . . er went to the UK funfair . . . at Jurong East . . . mmm . . . it was, it was interesting, but very expensive . . . erm the fun, the entrance fee is cheap, it's only two dollars
50		. . . I guess that's cheap enough, but then the . . . the the games and the rides are all very expensive,

		it's liked erm ... the cheapest ride I think is about three tokens that will be about ... eh, two-fifty per tokens, then about seven-fifty, wah, so it's pretty expensive ... for a ride, so in the end ... didn't didn't try out the rides so initially want to take the ferris wheel ... but then ... the queue is very long, and too expensive ((laughs)) so didn't, didn't take any ... spent about two hours there looking at the things ... very crowded ... mmm ... yah, then Sunday eh ... tried to do some reading up ... of erm ... the grammar modules, the one on functional functional grammar ... yah
100		took me the whole Sunday ... but didn't, but didn't manage to to to to ... er ... er how to say, finish the ... the readings ah ... mmm yup.
	Int	OK, so how was your three weeks experience teaching at a primary school, your posting?
	HM	Er ... three weeks ... er ... OK I guess, erm ... feel that um ... how to say ah ... er ... er didn't ... a lot of things to do lah, so didn't really enjoy the three weeks there ((laughs)) I guess it's because I know that I'm only be there for three weeks ... and um ... yah, so um ... mmm ...
150		er ... so don't know whether to um ... to put all my heart in there or ... or or or not, and then, erm ... yah ... then ... what else ... three weeks experience, er ... the class was all right, the the basically it's a good combination ah, of um um of children, the ... ba- the there are a few very good one, fast one, and there are extreme, there are also extreme slow ones, yeah, but basically the class ... is made up of ... a lot of, I mean kids from ... um broken families ... yah which require quite a lot of attention, not just academically, but um in other
200		areas ... yah, but I don't think I I I ... am able to give them that much in three weeks hor ... mmm ... so hopefully the teacher who took over ... the class would be able to provide more support ... for these children ... mmm, yah ... other than that, erm, colleagues-wise, I enjoy teaching in erm

250		Princess E . . . because erm most of them are very friendly, er the older teachers are pretty helpful, yah . . . they are just like, mmm . . . like like your your foster parents like that . . . yah . . . they're willing to share and er tell you about teaching and things like that . . . yeah, the younger ones . . . all all right also lah, I mean I have quite a few . . . friends over there who I know . . . mmm . . . yah, but I think currently the school that I'm posted to, Princess Elizabeth . . . I mean, the school has a lot of programmes going on this year that's why erm . . . that's why, erm I think most of the teacher who's working there now feels that they are very tied down with things other than teaching . . . yup, then um, like um they just had . . . they are going to have er E-topia, which is an open house, um IT open house, and then later on they're going to have their fiftieth anniversary . . . er celebration at the end of the year, in November, so there's a lot of things that the teachers need to be involved in, to prepare for these events, yup.

iF13-b

	Int	OK, um so what do you like to do during your free time?
	HM	OK, during my free time, first of all I want to have enough rest . . . yah, like . . . yah, enough rest, then um . . . then likely will be watch, watch more TV programmes, I guess, yah . . . mmm . . . but um, other than that, I would love to learn to . . . to cook, yah, because basically I don't know how to cook . . . yah, so I think, erm, I have wanted to do that . . . for quite some time already, but every time during the holidays, I'm too lazy to . . . to do it, and then my m- my mum will always says that never mind lah, next time when you get married,

50		you'll know how to cook ((laugh)) . . . so, um yeah lah, so only tried one or two dishes, didn't really do much cooking . . . other than that, I guess reading . . . yah, I'll do more more reading during the holidays, I mean leisure reading, like . . . reading the newspaper more . . . and then er magazines, yah magazines like Her World, or other magazines ah, any magazines . . . erm . . . and reading some fictions . . . erm, er will go down to the library to borrow some books . . . sometimes erm Chinese ones, English ones, yah . . . then, erm, other than that . . . mmm I will go cycling . . . yah, because during the holidays, like free time ah, erm yah, my m- . . . free time I guess is . . . during the holiday lah ((laughs)) that's why . . . so I guess I will try to go to the park to cycle because then I can go earlier, then it'll be, it won't be so crowded, yah . . . mmm . . . then, other than that . . . mmm . . . play with my niece and nephews . . . yup . . . bring them out, to the library, to the Sci- to Science Centre, times to the movies . . . ah . . . mmm . . . mm what else do I do during the free time?
100		
	Int	Just now you mentioned something about er reading, right? So did you subscribe any magazines?
150	HM	Magazines, OK, er I I . . . I didn't really subscribe any magazine previously . . . basically my sisters, they will buy . . . magazines like Her World, Cleo, er female magazines, yah, then I will just um . . . take the opportunity to to read them lah . . . yah er, but today I subscribed to three magazines, spent a lot of money on that, yah ((laughs)) . . . hopefully by subscribing to all these magazines I will read more widely . . . er, that is one reason why I want to subscribe to them . . . er subscribe to . . . three, one is Newsweek, National Geographic, and . . . World Environment . . . yah, I think they're quite . . . nice and interesting magazines . . . yah, hopefully I'll still believe in that after I've

200		((laughs)) after I've started on them . . . yup, mmm . . . yah, then nowadays, I mean nowadays, um, my sister just gave birth to a . . . a baby, my new nephew, he's only two months old, so I guess I will, my free time I'll I'll I'll . . . try to look after him, yah, play with him lah, mmm . . . mmm . . . other than that, yah, other than that, are things like going to the movies ah, yah, because during . . . school time hardly had time to watch any movies, mmm.
	Int	What are some of the . . . of the shows that you like?
250	HM	Mmm, I think . . . er I'll still prefer . . . English movies than Mandarin ones, because . . . Mandarin ones are like . . . like, no substance, I don't know how to say ((laugh)) no substance, yah, then, er, English movies I guess more varieties . . . maybe, yah, then, what kind of movies ah, I . . . suspense, cartoons even, er . . . what else . . . not scary ones, I guess, hardly watch any any horror movies, yup . . . seldom because most of the time I would not watch them, I will, I will cover my eyes ((laughs)) so I will waste my money ((laughs)) . . . erm, yah, basically that, yup . . . mmm, other than that, free time, eat lor, I guess . . . find time to eat, and at the same time do exercise . . . yah . . . yup . . . mmm yah that's all.

iF13-c

	Int	OK, so er which countries have you been to?
	HM	Erm, I have been to quite a few countries, er er erm . . . previously lah . . . these two years I've not . . . been travelling much because er, no income . . . but before that, um, most of the time I will go to one country at least for one, I mean, one country per year . . . yah so the first country I've, I mean the few country that I've been to are . . . erm . . .

Australia . . . Bali . . . erm Turkey . . . er Hong Kong . . . Taiwan . . . Korea, Japan, Nepal . . . er . . . yah, I think basically that . . . yup . . . mmm . . .

50 then, erm . . . and Malaysia lah, definitely, so for ((cough)) I think . . . I enjoy travelling, basically it's to um um . . . because I get to see other . . . um places . . . um and then um . . . enjoy the food there . . . and then um learn about the culture . . . mmm . . . so out of all these countries um . . . the trip to Turkey was quite . . . fun . . . it was er the first erm . . . the first trip that I had for . . . I mean for for thirteen days, yup, it's a long trip, yup, basically I was there for, with another friend, we were there on our own first for a few days before joining a . . . a local tour there . . . yup, so the first

100 few days we were just wandering around on our own, yup, and we met . . . the local people, and then um . . . yah they bring us around, it was quite . . . um interesting lah . . . then, erm . . . enjoyed the scenery there . . . yah . . . er and . . . shopping-wise, nothing much to buy there lah, basically . . . yup . . . then . . . mmm . . . the other trip I liked . . . was to Nepal, yah, because basically it's very scenic, yah and then the trekking, the rafting, all these and then, and the safari that we visit, all these are really erm very new to me, and erm . . .

150 yup, if I'm on my own I likely won't have tried them, yah, so the trekking . . . was fun . . . mmm . . . because I guess it wasn't that um . . . how to say ah, er it wasn't very . . . er dangerous, and it wasn't . . . it was quite relaxing, because the the the . . . the . . . sherpa, they call it . . . they were very helpful, and, yah, so we were walking at our own pace, yup . . . yup, then rafting was fun, exciting, yah, then erm . . . the safari was . . . interesting also, basically we ss- we we went on treks to look for animals, yah

200 like rhino, erm yah sat on elephant's back, yup, to to move around the jungle, mmm . . . OK ((cough)) would have wanted to go back to Nepal again but I guess, as I grow older I doubt I can er

250	Int HM	do that kind of trekking ((laughs)) erm yah, I guess the most recent trip will be to . . . to Japan . . . yup . . . Japan is . . . mmm . . . OK lah, the countryside is . . . is nice, yup, erm . . . the the cities is really very crowded . . . very crowded . . . yup, won't enjoy, I don't think, if I really want to go back to Japan I won't want to go back to the city . . . yah. Cities? Which ones? Like Tokyo and er Osaka . . . mmm . . . a lot of people there, yah . . . then, mmm, when you go into the trains, usually you will be . . . squashed . . . ((laughs)) during the early hours lah, when they are on their wa-, when they are g-, when there are a lot of people going to work, yah . . . mmm . . . what, er . . . think, other than that, Australia is a . . . nice place to go to also, I guess it's . . . erm, very easy to move around, because they speak English, yup . . . mmm . . . mmm Taiwan . . . OK lah, er how to say . . . er . . . er . . . nothing, nothing impressed me over there . . . yup . . . yeah lah.

iF13-d

50	Int HM	OK, just now you said you have been to Australia, can you tell me more about Australia? Mmm, Australia, I've been to Sydney . . . and Perth . . . yup . . . er the trip to Sydney was . . . um only for a few days with a group of friends . . . yah actually we were there for some . . . church ac-activity, basically, but other than that we will go sightseeing, yah, so, erm . . . mmm, that was my first trip oversea, yah, so actually I enjoyed the experience, on the plane and then um over at Australia also . . . erm, yah, the people . . . OK lah I guess I didn't really, erm . . . erm because it was really a big group . . . um of us, a really huge group, so um . . . didn't really erm . . . mmm we'll

		move around in one big group lor, yah, so didn't really interact much with the local people there . . . but other than that, mmm . . . OK lor, the place . . . mmm while for Perth, I was there with my sister . . . and . . . my brother-in-law, yah, just the three of us, and erm we join a tour lah, I mean . . . erm . . . with a a a tour agency over here, so, that trip was all right, mmm Perth is a very er quiet place, I guess . . . I'll I'll say it's a very easy-going, quiet place definitely can go on your own . . . yah, then um, we were there for about six days . . . then erm, the . . . you can move around on your own very easily, erm . . . mmm . . . the people there . . . are OK, it seems liked erm they take life very easy over there ((laughs)) . . . and then er, other than that we actually went to Fremantle . . . ss-Fremantle, yah . . . erm it's a quiet, another quiet town, yah, a small one . . . yup ((cough)) didn't do much shopping over there, basically just walking, looking at the place . . . they do have shopping area lah, yah . . . but not really like big shopping centre . . . mmm . . . mmm . . . yup.
100		
	Int	So is there anywhere else you would like to go?
150	HM	Mmm . . . I guess Europe is one place, because I only been to Turkey, yah, only Turkey, basically Turkey . . . erm Europe, like erm Switzerland, erm France, erm . . . a lot lah, Germany, Austria . . . yah, any place you name, I guess.
	Int	((laughs))
	HM	Yup, but I guess it's really expensive, to go over to Europe and erm to visit so many places, yah . . . so . . . other than Europe, erm . . . mmm China maybe hor, yah . . . er likely lah, one of these days will will will go to China . . . yup, mmm . . . other than these two areas . . . last time I would want to go to down to Africa . . . yah, mmm, but I don't know about now, don't have the enthusiasm.
200		
	Int	Why not?
	HM	((laughs)) Don't know, I guess it's like erm . . . don't

	Int	know ah, just want to find a place that is erm easy to ((laughs)) travel, I don't think Australia can go, um er no, um um South Africa can go on your own . . . I guess you, it will be better to be guided, yup. So you like free-and-easy tours?
	HM	Yah, I do, I prefer free-and-easy to . . . er guided ones, because you can move on your own, er whatev-, I mean, you don't have to follow the time schedule of your tour guide, yup . . . mmm, mmm . . . eh . . . mmm other . . .
250	Int	So which, which country in Europe are you erm interested, most interested in going?
	HM	Mmm, most interested ah, my first choice ah . . . . ahhh erm . . . maybe Switzerland . . . yah again, I guess what attracts me is that it's scenic, the mountains, yah, and then the ((tsk)) er . . . yah, I guess s-, basically it's because it's scenic lah . . . yah, I think one place that I can compare with Switzerland easily is New Zealand, I always feel that these two places . . . erm look pretty the same, to me ((laughs))
	Int	Have you ever been there?
	HM	No, I've never been to New Zealand, maybe that will be a, a b- . . . a cheaper . . . place to go, compared to Switzerland . . . yah.

iF13-e

	Int	OK, so is teaching your first job?
	HM	Mmm . . . not really, er . . . no, not really, it's it's definitely no ((laughs)) er my first job was um working as a . . . what do you call that . . . um engineering assistant at the . . . manufacturing company . . . yup, basically I was erm erm . . . I I I did electronic engineering . . . before that, so after that I was um . . . posted ah, I don't think called posted lah, but um, I signed this contract with a . . . manufac- with this c- manufacturing company

50		to work there for three years . . . yup . . . so, erm . . . this company deals with . . . I mean, um, manufacture . . . video-cassette recorders . . . yah, it's under Thomson and Toshiba, yup, so, um, I was there, my main job . . . was to plan and erm . . . plan production lines . . . yah, and then erm . . . erm write out write out the procedures for making erm VCR . . . yup . . . so will will have to write out as in how to assemble the VCR to . . . testing it to packing it, yah, so the whole process I need to break down for the different operators . . . and erm within the specific time limit per station . . . yup . . . other than that, erm, at times, after, I mean, um there will be, um, I will have to do, um . . . projects like improving the line, as in er cutting down the
100		number of . . . headcounts, yup, for er certain models, so as to save cost, yah, erm . . . mmm . . . so, this job basically there will be, erm, there are times when you are very busy, and there are times when it's erm . . . mmm mmm . . . not as busy lah, yah, so er the busy time will be when there's there are many new models, yah, so you have to test them out, on the line when the production is not running so you have to work off-time, to check, to test the station . . . yah . . . and then erm . . . mmm then liaise with the erm . . . the . . . R and D department with any problems that you encounter . . . yah . . . so, mmm . . . mmm worked there for . . . six . . . and a half years, I guess about
150		there, the first three years was bonded so after that, didn't wanted to . . . go anywhere, so stayed on ((laugh))with the company . . . for another three years yah, until, until . . . it shut down ((laugh)) basically I was retrenched, but before I was retrenched I actually applied for teaching already, so it's not because of I I was out of a job, then I applied teaching, yah . . . mmm.
	Int	So is this the reason why you chose the teaching profession?
	HM	Mmm, not really, actually I considered before

200		coming in, into teaching, I mean before erm signing up, I actually thought of being a librarian . . . and teaching is the other option ah, so erm, I actually went for interviews, erm, before I got retrenched, I actually went for interviews with um, National Library Board I mean with um Nanyang Pol-, oh no, Temasek Poly, yah, to work in the library, their libraries, but erm . . . er they actually advised me not to, because they feel that er with my qualification, having a diploma in electronic engineering, you shouldn't work in the library as just a normal . . . erm librarian, because they only they only consider only my . . . 'A' Levels . . . yah, one thing the pay will be very low . . . another thing you'll be doing something very simple, basically yah, so erm . . . then erm, yah, when after that, erm, considered teaching, so . . . I guess why I chose teaching . . . it could be because er, I I . . . wanted something different, I wanted something . . . more challenging, it's definitely very challenging . . . and er, working with people, I was thinking, erm . . . you'll be, you you will feel more satisfaction . . . so called ah, other than working with products, you know, just . . . just . . . trying to . . . produce more VCR every day . . . yah, so . . . yah, that's why I chose teaching . . . yah . . . mmm . . . erm . . . other than that, erm . . . mmm I guess . . . er, other than satisfaction . . . erm.
250		
	Int	Do you like children?
	HM	Oh, I like children a lot, er . . . OK, I guess, I won't say I will, I love them a lot, but er, I I . . . I do enjoy talking to them at times lah, yah, er yup but . . . OK lah I guess . . . erm.

iF13-f

	Int	OK, um, so is there anything you like about this new campus?
	HM	Er, this new campus, I guess, mmm . . . I guess I like the library the most, yah, it it's it it really is erm very different from the old library . . . yup . . . and then erm . . . more, more tables . . . and chairs, I mean, more more . . . tables and chairs ((laugh)) for students ((laughs)) . . . erm, other than that erm, and then er, and they're going to set up a . . . cafe in the library, that is good also . . . erm . . . yup, then erm . . .
	Int	How often do you think you'll go to the cafe ((laughs))?
50	HM	How often ah . . . I don't know, it depends how often I stay in the library, yeah lah, that depends, I guess . . . before I graduate I'll definitely er visit there a few times, right . . . yah, mmm . . . erm ((cough)) then erm . . . other than the library, mmm . . . I guess I like . . . what, I mean all the rooms are new, the tutorial rooms are new, and er . . . the aircons are . . . it's always working, compared to the old campus, yup . . . mmm . . . mmm . . .
	Int	The lecture halls?
	HM	O- Lecture halls . . . all right lah, compared to the old, old lecture halls we have . . . er . . . OK I guess, no special feelings towards them . . . yah ((laugh))
100		but I guess what I don't like about the school is the canteen, it's too small . . . previously we have th- . . . about three canteens, I think three, ah, three canteens, so . . . i- it give to you, I don't know whether are they really big or not compared to this one, but I guess it give you the feeling that you have more options to go to, I mean just, not just one . . . one canteen, yah . . . but this one is like . . . it's like every time . . . during lunch time especially from twelve-thirty to one-thirty it will be very crowded . . . yup . . . then erm . . . mmm . . .

150		then the queues will be very long, there's no place for you to stand . . . actually . . . yah . . . then mmm . . . but comparing this campus with the old campus, I think I like the old campus in the sense, it has its unique . . . look lor, I don't know how to say, it's really erm . . . old and then . . . erm, you feel comfortable there . . . yah . . . mmm . . . maybe I'm old also lah, that's why ((laughs)) . . . I feel I ((laugh)) belong there ((laughs)) . . . er . . . what else
	Int	But is it more accessible? I mean which one is more accessible?
200	HM	Oh yah, definitely the old campus is more accessible . . . yup . . . the new one, this new one is like, you have to take a feeder from, from Boon Lay and you have to wait . . . for the bus, it's definitely . . . mmm . . . erm not as accessible as compared to the old one, the old one . . . erm, though it seems like I I stay in Clementi and then Jurong seems nearer, but I think I take long, a longer time to reach here than erm, to to go, to get down to the old campus . . . yup . . . yah . . . mmm . . . then . . . mmm . . . erm . . . what else . . . then I guess, mmm . . . let me ((laughs)) . . . OK, er, let me think, what I . . . can't think of anything.
	Int	OK, just now you mentioned about reading, er what kind of books do you. . . do you like to read?
250	HM	What kind ((laughs)) of books . . . I guess, erm . . . reading ah, I guess, erm . . . mmm fictions, fictions, erm . . . actually, non, yah I mean erm, at times I do read romance . . . stories . . . erm, but I guess . . . as you grow older, I think I like more . . . non-fiction books . . . erm, most likely biographies of people . . . yah, I will enjoy those books also . . . yup, mmm . . . mmm, I guess so . . . mmm . . . er . . . magazines ah, magazines . . . er . . . mmm . . . all sorts lah, I guess I would try to read . . . all kinds of . . . magazines . . . yah . . . er . . . hopefully I'll enjoy, actually subscribe Newsweek, right, yah, hopefully I'll enjoy, reading it . . . mmm.

iF13-g

	Int	OK, er why did you take up er English and maths as your AS?
	HM	Mmm . . . erm . . . I guess why I chose English is because I erm . . . I mean, why I chose English when I came into NIE is because I think I will, it, I think being a teacher I need to be able to speak well, write well in English, so as to communicate with my students, so that's why I chose English as . . . the first AS, yah, to do in NIE, then for maths, I guess I did A-Level maths so . . . erm it'll be easier for me to do maths, yah, at NIE, as compared to taking up geography or history or literature which
50		I had little, erm . . . knowledge of . . . yah, so I chose maths and . . . maths basically is about doing tutorials, and erm it's a very systematic way in in doing the modules . . . yah, so . . . I'm comfortable with the, with the method lah . . . the way of erm . . . yah . . . so that's why I chose these two . . . modules . . . yup . . . these two AS . . . mmm . . . yah, then later on, I decided to choose English as the one to major rather than maths . . . it's because . . . I feel that English, again I feel that English is more . . . useful . . . in daily life, so erm . . . that's why I chose English and not maths, because maths
100		is getting more and more abstract . . . yah, and erm . . . if I'm going to teach in a primary school I feel that maybe English would be more appropriate . . . to . . . major in than maths . . . yah . . . then another thing is that . . . choosing English as . . . my major, I'll have fewer modules to do . . . yah er, yah . . . that's why . . . erm . . . yah, that's w- another reason ah . . . mmm . . . then . . .
	Int	So is there a possibility that they're going to post you in secondary schools?
	HM	Mmm . . . so far . . . I mean everyone have beens talk- have beens . . . talking about it, whether you'll be posted to secondary school or JC . . . well I guess . . . there could be . . . erm . . . yah, it it may,

150		I may be posted to secondary school, but erm . . . see how, I guess, if I decided to teach in a primary school I may, I may erm . . . go and approach a school, a few schools . . . to talk to the principal and see whether I could teach in that school or not . . . yah, so as to get a place . . . for myself lah in primary school, rather than secondary school . . . because I guess I'm still a bit wary about teaching English in secondary school, yah . . . maybe teaching maths is . . . OK . . . for secondary school maths . . . yah, but English . . . I'm still not confident in . . . in yah in teaching English, I mean, not confident in teaching English in primary s- er in secondary school . . . mmm.
200	Int HM	So will you request to go back to Princess E? Erm . . . mmm going back to Princess Elizabeth . . . that's the primary school I'm posted to, right . . . er . . . I don't know . . . seriously, I I guess I don't know, now . . . at the moment, I feel that I won't want, I mmm likelihood I would not request . . . to go back . . . er the other time I didn't request, after my degree programme I didn't actually request to any primary school but I was posted to Princess E . . . erm after that . . . so um, this time round, I guess I likelihood I would not request back again . . . because there may be change of plans, I may be um . . . I may be getting married ((laughs)), so er likelihood I may not, I may not be staying in the west . . . yah, so by requesting back, it's like erm, you will have to stay at the school for five years, I
250		guess . . . and I don't think it's very nice to erm, after, I mean, after teaching there for a year and you request for a change . . . yah . . . so I guess I'll rather not request back there . . . mmm though I do, will miss the teachers there lah, I mean . . . most of the teachers there are very helpful and nice . . . nice people . . . mmm . . . yah.
	Int	When you mentioned that, if the need arise, you will request for a primary school . . . so which school are you interested?

	HM	So far I have not erm . . . really 1- think about it . . . but I guess I will, when times come maybe in January I will talk to a few of my friends who are already posted out . . . teaching in schools . . . then er, in the north side, likelihood, I will erm ask them about how, how are their schools ah . . . then erm, maybe if I really want to I will go down and . . . see them and talk to the principal, yup.

iF13-h

	Int	Aiya, why do you want to take up the Honours course?
	HM	Er, why ah, I guess . . . mmm . . . by taking this up I'll earn more ((laughs)) . . . the salary scale will definitely be better . . . yah, erm that is one reason, another reason I guess, being offered, I just want to take the opportunity to try . . . yah . . . and erm, I mean before that, when I was doing my degree, I I did think of . . . I mean, I did, I did, I did erm think of just fin- I mean . . . stop studying after my, I mean my degree programme . . . been tired a bit, I mean, tired of t- studying already, so erm that's why . . . I mean, erm . . . but then, after being offered, it's like, changed my mind and erm . . .
50		was thinking, OK, just try lah . . . yah, then quite a few of my friends are in here also . . . doing their Honours . . . yah, so I mean there are, there are companies ah . . . I have companies with me so I guess . . . er won't be so lonely, and then erm, we can still help one another to, to . . . in this programme ah, yah . . . then erm . . . mmm hopefully this one year, will learn a, learn more things . . . and um, yah, before going out to teach, for life, I guess ((laughs)) . . . er . . . mmm.
	Int	So do you think you'll stay in your teaching career for life?
	HM	Mmm . . . staying in here, I guess, till now my

100		mindset is yah, I will . . . because this is already my second job . . . yah . . . I I I won't say career, I don't know far I can go, but I guess it's my second job and erm . . . I doubt I will switch again . . . I already had a big . . . jump, I mean big . . . big big change . . . from engineering to teaching, yah, it's totally different, so erm after studying, I think including this year of Honours, I'll have, I would have five years with NIE . . . another five years of bond after that, and I don't think I want to . . . start something new again and learn something . . . new, I guess, so teaching will be . . . a lifetime thing ah, but it's whether after the five years, five years, five-year bond . . . will I want to stop . . . I mean erm . . . teaching in schools but go into tuitions . . . or or . . . private teaching or what I don't know, maybe, but . . . first thing . . . I mean for now, it's definitely I hope to stay as long as possible . . . in teaching, that means I need to enjoy teaching, I need to be able to teach well also . . . because . . . till now I still feel that I lack the ability to teach well . . . first of all, it's in managing the class . . . I guess that is really very important . . . if you can't manage a class . . . you can't really teach . . . yah . . . so that's one thing that I need to brush up on . . . yah . . . yup . . . mmm, teaching is definitely very challenging.
150		
	Int	So out of like the few subjects, English, maths, science or arts, what is your favourite?
200	HM	My favourite subject to teach ah . . . aiya ((tsk)) . . . don't know lah, I guess . . . mmm . . . I thought maths would be something easy to teach, because . . . it's fixed . . . I mean it's pretty fixed lor, compared to English that is quite . . . er . . . living, you call it living . . . yah, so erm . . . yah, so I thought maths was . . . would be easier . . . while for science . . . it's like er you need to read widely, because students can just ask any questions about . . . anything, yah, and erm . . . I guess I I I still lack . . . erm the ability to answer questions . . .

250		spontaneously, so called . . . yup, so erm . . . which subject ah . . . I guess I have no preference now, I hope I will enjoy teaching all, all of them as in English, maths and science, while for arts, mmm . . . I guess arts, OK lah, one thing I can enjoy, I mean maybe I will like arts is that it's not exam, it it's, that's, it's not . . . there's no exam, you know things like that, but erm teaching lower primary arts is quite all right, they are k- still . . . they still like arts . . . but erm upper primary I guess need to motivate them more . . . um and then and that require you to be able . . . you yourself being enthusiastic about the subject, in order to influence others, mmm . . . to enjoy it also.

iF13-i

	Int	What sports would you like to pick up?
	HM	Sports, mmm . . . I guess . . . er, one sp- . . . one would be rollerblading . . . yah, erm, I mean I've seen people rollerblading in the park, it seems like an easy sport, if you know it, yah, so . . . but I guess the tough thing would be . . . learning it, learning it at the beginning lah, and erm . . . buying the the the equipment . . . would be quite expensive also, yah . . . so, but it seems . . . erm . . . yah I mean, I see people blading, blading . . . in the park like leisurely, it's really fun, yup . . . so that is one thing that I may want to pick it up, during the holidays
50		yah, not now, definitely not now ((laughs)) . . . yah, then erm, swimming maybe, yah erm . . . didn't really have a chance to learn swimming properly, so if I can, I would hope to learn swimming . . . I guess it's a very good sports . . . to master, not to master lah, but to be able to participate in . . . yup . . . it i- erm . . . previously I had, I had swimming lessons at erm . . . ACJC, during my JC time, yah

		we had erm PE, erm . . . w- once . . . once a week,
		or once in two weeks, yah we have to go down to
		HCJ, A t-, ACS, yah, to use the pool for swimming
		lessons, yah, but that time, didn't really take that
		opportunity to to learn it, and er just go there for
100		fun and then erm . . . yah, and then . . . didn't . . .
		didn't really practise other than . . . that that two
		hours or less than two hours there, yah . . . then
		there was once I erm . . . almost get drowned, not
		drowned basically, open inverted comma lah,
		basically it's that er, but I learnt to use, I learnt to
		kick, bas- basically the lect- the instructor taught
		us how to erm do freestyle . . . maybe he shouldn't
		have, should have taught me to do frogstyle first,
		so, so we learnt to kick, float after that learnt to
		kick, you know after that, learnt how to erm the
		the the how to use our hands, the motions of our
		hands, I don't know what you call that, yah . . .
		then, he just say 'OK, put them all together and
150		swim across the pool', so ((laughs)) that's what we
		try, I try, so when I do it I couldn't coordinate at
		all, when I kick my hands doesn't move, when I
		when I move my hands, my my feet stop kicking,
		so basically I I . . . so basically I sink lah ((laughs)),
		so I struggle . . . basically it's just er me . . . i- i- it's
		not the the deep pool you know . . . so it's very
		embarrassing, I I couldn't get my feet on the . . . on
		the ground so in the end the the instructor has to
		. . . jumped in and then erm . . . pick me up, mmm
		. . . so after that I think I have a phobia . . . going to
		the pool, yah . . . so I think because of that I didn't
		manage to learn swimming . . . yup . . . so, mmm
		other than that . . . mmm . . . er do, did visit the
		swimming pool a few times, the public swimming
200		pools, but erm yah, didn't really dare to swim lah
		. . . yup, so till now still don't know how to swim,
		mmm . . . er . . . other than . . . swimming,
		rollerblading, tennis, maybe tennis, I have learnt
		tennis before, so it's basically to pick it up again
		. . . yah, so um um, tennis is something that I

250		enjoyed doing also, I mean that time . . . er nowadays hardly had a chance, to play tennis, badminton . . . I mean I I I play that also, just that erm, you need to get a few players in order to to to . . . play it, yah . . . so erm, squash . . . yah . . . I, isn't it, all these torp- sports I did a bit a bit a bit . . . of a bit of them during um . . . um um previously ah, so erm, after that I, I will stop and then didn't continue, so squash is another one that I have tried before . . . and it's fun, especially when you have a lot of . . . when you're very angry, you have stress, that's ((laugh)) the ((laugh)) place to ((laugh)) to, that's the place to go . . . yah, erm . . . squash . . . er . . . skating, ice-skating, it looks to me a very dangerous sport . . . yah because the blade looks so sharp, I mean it's like if you fall another person will will will will ((laugh)) may just, erm, how to say ((laugh)), may just erm cut you with their their blades when they erm . . . er move past you . . . yah.

iF13-j

	Int	Er, have you been to Pulau Ubin?
50	HM	Yah, I've been to Pulau Ubin . . . a few times . . . erm . . . I guess er twice I was there cycling, with um friends, yup, first time, yah, I mean not first time . . . both times, when I were there . . . um um cycling . . . er I was, I shared a bike with a friend, that means a double-bike, yah, basically . . . doub-yah, correct, double-bike . . . and then erm another time I was there, just . . . visiting the place . . . had some . . . had . . . er a small . . . picnic there, I guess you call that a picnic ((laugh)) . . . yah . . . but it was a nice place to go to, very quiet, serene . . . serene, yah, and erm . . . it . . . mmm I enjoyed being there lah, other than the mosquitoes . . . mmm . . . so erm . . . er . . . mmm what else . . .

		Int	Recently they just discovered this Chek Jawa, have you been there?
		HM	Er, no, I've not been there, I've heard of my friends talking about it, and I've seen, I've seen pictures of it also, and actually I would like to visit there one day, and erm, yah, because I, but I think it's not easy to . . . just go there on your own, you need to book . . . the place and things like that, yah, get arrange erm erm . . . for a tour guide to bring you, is er, yah . . . so . . . yah if I have the opportunity I would want to visit there one, one of these days . . . yup . . . mmm . . . there are, they have chalets at Pulau Ubin also, maybe next time if really . . . got no place to go to, then I'll go ((laughs)), I'll go there for . . . stay I guess.
100		Int	So have you been to other islands?
		HM	Other islands . . . erm, yah, the common ones will be Sentosa . . . yah, that's one place that I've been to quite er . . . quite frequently, I mean not frequently nowadays but previously lah . . . yah now Sentosa has been . . . I mean erm . . . fewer and fewer people visit Sentosa I guess . . . especially after the Fantasy Island . . . has been closed . . . down . . . and erm, I've been there the other time . . . yah, it was very quiet, very few people were there . . . yah . . . basically tourist lah, some tourists . . . yah . . . other than Sentosa I've been to . . . Kusu Island recently . . . er it's a very small island . . . I can't remember how big it is but it's really small . . . er it's . . . it, I take a ferry, from . . . from World Trade Centre, and it's about mmm half-an-hour journey . . . I guess it's about half-an-hour journey, from World Trade to Kusu Island, yup, and um . . . over there, there's only that, the, basically people go there . . . to visit the temple I guess, especially during . . . erm . . . September . . . September October, when most Chinese will go there . . . for the temple, you'll see big crowds there . . . er when it comes to September . . . so there is one Chinese temple . . . and one Malay
150			

200 250		shrine, yah they call it a shrine, I didn't visit the Malay shrine, it's erm . . . up on a small . . . lump of . . . ((laughs)) . . . g- I I mean it's um . . . ((laugh)) what, OK OK, anyway, um . . . that day when I was there it was very quiet, quiet also, maybe it's because it's a week day . . . yup, a week day . . . and erm . . . they d- . . . I like places that is quiet lah, so I I I enjoyed my day there, I had a picnic there . . . so erm erm . . . there's a small, there there is a lagoon . . . there also . . . yah and s- a . . . a beach ah, I guess, there's a beach there, mmm . . . so basically just sit down there and have picnic, yah . . . er . . . but the . . . erm . . . during weekdays there're only . . . how many ferri-, how many trips there, I think . . . one trip is at ten . . . in the morning, followed by . . . one-thirty . . . something like that, only two trips . . . yup . . . yah, actually the ferry will fetch people to Kusu Island and then to St John Island . . . and then um . . . after that, back to World Trade . . . yah, maybe the next . . . island I will want to visit could be St John Island, it's a bigger island . . . they have chalets there and things like that, I think most . . . s- most people will go to St John rather than Kusu Island . . . mmm . . . yup.

iF13-k

	Int HM	Erm, would you like to tell me more about your family? Er, my family . . . OK, um basically, mmm . . . my, I mean, in my family I have my parents, and then um, I have . . . myself and four other sibling . . . siblings, yup, so I'm the eldest at home, and I have . . . three other sisters and a youngest brother, yup, so um, all of us already, I mean . . . except myself, the rest of them are already um . . . um completed their studying, so all of them are working, yup,

50	then er two of my sisters, they're already married, their own family, so I have erm . . . a few . . . I have two nephews, and one niece, basically . . . yup . . . erm . . . then erm . . . so er my my sister, one of my sister . . . she actually stayed next door to to us, so erm, so that it's easier for my niece and nephew to go to s- to a nearby school . . . um, in our area so that my mum will be able take care of them, when um they finish s- finish school . . . erm yah, because both my sister and brother-in-law works . . . work . . . so erm it will be easier for my mother to take care of them, so erm last year they decided to shift down from, Choa Chu Kang to, yah to our area, mmm . . . yup . . . then my niece is er K-, in
100	K2, next year she'll be going to Primary One . . . yup, my nephew, erm my my my older e- nephew is in Primary Four this year . . . yah, so erm . . . my niece will be studying in the same school as him lah next year . . . mmm . . . then erm my, I just have er, I mean er my sister just gave birth to a baby . . . so my new nephew, he is only two months old, yah, so . . . my mum is looking after him also, for my sister . . . mmm . . . yah, so he will stay at our place, erm during the weekdays, and then he will go home for the weekends, mmm . . . erm . . . then other than that, erm . . . my . . .
150	other than my parents and my siblings, erm, my grandmother, my aunt and uncle also stay next door . . . so erm yah, so erm . . . at times my . . . erm . . . at times my grandmother will come over to our place . . . yah, after taking her lunch . . . or dinner, mmm . . . when um, yah . . . so . . . so basically most of my family members stay around . . . us, stay around me lah, yah, erm . . . mmm . . . er . . . my brother, he, he has signed on with SAF, so he
200	mmm he's he he seldom stays at home because he will stay in camp . . . at times . . . mmm . . . then, er . . . er . . . normally, erm, normally OK, my dad and my m-, my dad has retired, so he will stay at home with my mother to look after my nephews and

250		niece, yup, other than looking after them, he will erm, he has his erm . . . erm pets and erm . . . and erm . . . flowering to do, he he he he . . . er he's keeping a few fish . . . nowadays, yah you heard of luo-han-yu, I don't know what you call that in English, yah, so he's keeping two of . . . two of that, yah, one big one and one small one, one baby one, yah, other than that, he . . . he do some . . . er . . . pen-zai ah, bonsai ah, you call that, yah . . . er he will . . . he he, so he will spend time watering them, um . . . and erm . . . yah, something like that, previously he actually kept cuckoo birds ((laughs)) so um, just two weeks ago he he he . . . he stopped . . . he gave away quite a few, initially he has five . . . OK, and then he gave away the most expensive one to someone and then now he's only looking after two . . . yah, the rest he actually let them go . . . mmm.

iF13-I

50	HM	Erm, OK, erm so I . . . my mum usually erm . . . most of, nowadays she . . . she look after my niece and nephews yah, last time . . . erm . . . she will um babysit for other people, yah when erm . . . all of us, as in myself and my sisters and brothers er were studying, yah still studying, so . . . she will have additional income by babysitting other people's erm . . . children, yup, so erm . . . yah, that was like a long way back, when I was in primary school, yah . . . so, erm nowadays some of the kids that she have brought up, actually do keep in to-contact with her, yah, and at times they will come and visit her, during Chinese New Year . . . mmm . . . so nowadays, erm . . . she will have to look after . . . erm . . . my niece and nephews, so usually erm . . . my n- . . . usually she will erm . . . get ready erm the meals for them, send them to school, so

		with my new nephew now, the baby nephew at home, my dad will have to help up . . . by erm bringing my niece to school in the morning and bringing her back, from kindergarten, yah . . . then erm . . . my dad may help to do, may help in the marketing side, marketing part . . . by going to the market to get some . . . erm the things that she need lor . . . yah, oth- if not erm, she will do fewer trips to the market . . . have fewer trips to market lah, every week . . . not like last time . . . mmm . . .
100		while at home, she will look after the baby, basically it's to feed and wash him . . . at erm specific times, and then erm . . . at night, she will have to feed the baby also, yah, every three-hourly she will have to wake up . . . to to feed the baby . . . mmm . . . erm . . . yah . . . then erm, other than that . . . er.
	Int	So won't it be very noisy with the baby around? How are you going to study?
	HM	Oh . . . erm . . . OK I guess, I guess I'm used to having children . . . at my place, you know, since long time ago, yah, so till now the baby is still not so bad lah, because basically . . . he will cry when
150		he he he need food . . . or attention, but er he doesn't cry the whole day, mmm . . . so not so bad . . . but er, yah . . . I guess noise is not a problem . . . mmm . . . er yup . . . I guess the problem is when I, I'm too tired to study I'll play with the baby, then ((laugh)) I won't want to study . . . so, that will be the distraction rather than the noise ((laughs)) . . . yah . . . yeah lah . . . erm . . .
	Int	So you said you would like to learn cooking, um you mean you're going to learn it from your mother?
	HM	Mmm . . . yah, I tried learning from my mother . . . yah, a few dishes lah, so far . . . mmm . . . but erm . . . my mum didn't really like me to . . . to learn
200		from her I guess it's because she doesn't want me to meddle with the kitchen, and then dirty the place . . . so erm . . . so that's why . . . that's also one

250		excuse I have that I I I'm not learning it now ((laughs)) . . . yah . . . but I guess I'll start with my mum if I really want to cook . . . yah, and then I mean I w-, I can try out a few recipes . . . yah, from those recipe books, mmm . . . previously I do bake quite a lot . . . with my sisters when we, when um, I mean, many years ago when all of us are still together, mmm . . . erm, when erm . . . no-one has married off yet . . . so, that time we would actually baking . . . bake . . . cakes . . . make cookies . . . yah, with the oven at home, but erm . . . since the oven is spoilt . . . we stopped baking and er . . . making cookies, yup . . . so, but my sister bought a oven . . . when she shifted to the new house, so at times erm she will bake . . . er and make cookies ah, erm during Chinese New Year we will gather together and make cookies also at her place, mmm . . . yup . . . mmm . . .
	Int	Your sister, you mean the one staying next door?
	HM	No, not the one staying next door, but the one erm . . . the other one, yah . . . the one next door only had a mini, small . . . oven, I don't know whether, yah, so cannot, cannot do cooking, I mean cannot really bake cake ah . . . yup . . . mmm, yah . . . so, yeah lah.

Index